More Books
by Donald Spellman

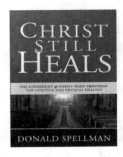

Christ Still Heals—Does Christ still heal? Author Donald Spellman emphatically says yes in his book *Christ Still Heals: The Atonement of Christ Made Provision for Spiritual and Physical Healing.* In this book, readers learn how the atonement of Christ provided not only for spiritual healing but physical healing as well. *Christ Still Heals* is filled with plenty of biblical case studies of God healing His people, including Apostle Spellman's personal testimonies.

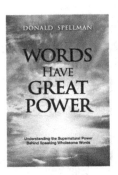

In Words Have Great Power, you will learn what the Bible says about words and how they can affect you, including how blessings and curses come from your words. Apostle Spellman explains the root problem of an uncontrollable tongue and the steps you can take to be healed. If you want to build up others as well as yourself, journey through this book to explore how your words can edify and strengthen those around you.

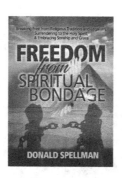

There are multitudes of well-meaning believers in Christ who have a distorted assessment of God the Father. Instead of knowing Him as loving, holy, righteous, and compassionate Father, they see Him as a tyrant who enforces fabricated religious rules and their denominational agendas, and who is not concerned about their spiritual well-being. My friend, Jesus came to set the captives free, and today He's still setting free those who desire to be liberated. *Freedom from Spiritual Bondage* does not simply expose religion and legalism for what they are; it offers the antithesis to spiritual bondage—the grace of the Lord Jesus in its place, backed by Scriptural context.

Do you feel trapped or engulfed by religious legalism? Are you desiring a meaningful relationship with the Lord rather than a checklist of rules? This book is for you. Spellman discusses how there are multitudes of Christians who think it's okay to habitually sin because God's grace is accessible in the person of Christ Jesus.

There are many profound books written on the subject of grace, but Spellman is prayerful that this book will reaffirm the richness and beauty of grace. God's grace is absolutely magnificent; no amount of pages, pamphlets, books, lectures, songs, or messages can do justice to or express the wealth and depth of His unmerited favor.

GOD'S COMPASSION NEVER FAILS

DAILY DEVOTIONS FILLED WITH ENCOURAGEMENT, COMFORT, AND HOPE

DONALD SPELLMAN

WESTBOW
PRESS®
A DIVISION OF THOMAS NELSON
& ZONDERVAN

WestBow Press books may be ordered through booksellers or by contacting:

WestBow Press
·A Division of Thomas Nelson & Zondervan
1663 Liberty Drive
Bloomington, IN 47403
www.westbowpress.com
844-714-3454

ISBN: 979-8-3850-1612-9 (sc)
ISBN: 979-8-3850-1613-6 (hc)
ISBN: 979-8-3850-1630-3 (e)

Library of Congress Control Number: 2024900289

Print information available on the last page.

WestBow Press rev. date: 02/02/2024

✧ ✧ ✧

Through the Lord's mercies we are not consumed, because
His compassions fail not. They are new every morning; Great
is Your faithfulness. The Lord is my portion, says my soul,
therefore I hope in Him! The Lord is good to those who
wait for Him. To the soul who seeks Him. It is good that one
should hope and wait quietly, for the salvation of the Lord.

—Lamentations 3:22–26

CONTENTS

II.   Proclamations and Confessions

III. Prayers, Petitions, and Spiritual Warfare Prayers

ACKNOWLEDGMENTS

With immense gratitude I give honor, praise, and glory to my Lord and Savior Jesus Christ! It's because of Him I move, live, and have my being. Without Christ, I can do nothing; but with Him I'm able to do all things because He strengthens me. To my beautiful wife, Sheila, of thirty-eight years, I appreciate all your love and support, and your being a great mother to our four grown sons. I love you profoundly; may God continue to favor and bless you!

I would like to thank some people who have been very supportive of Living Word of Grace Ministries, Healing Ministry Broadcasts, and Book Ministry. A special thanks to WestBow Press (Publisher), Michael Spellman (Spellman's Computers), the staff of WMOC 88.7 FM (Lumber City, Georgia), Facebook live stream c/o Eddie Wmoc Inspirator Conaway, Terrance Roberson (site manager, Detention Center, North Carolina), Evangelist Shirley Spellman, Mary S. Liverman, Tyrone Spellman, Deacon Tony Gibson, Sister Elaine Brown, Pastor Steven Butler, Prophet Adair Johnson, Apostle Dr. James Brewton, Dr. Dale Miles, and Prophet Rodney Wilkens. With no special order of precedence, I thank you and everyone whom I fail to mention for your heartfelt support and prayers.

PREFACE

It's a no-brainer after reading the gospel accounts of Matthew, Mark, Luke, and John that Christ came to seek and save that which is lost. Although this was His primary mission, addressing the needs of those He came in contact with was a high priority as well. While on earth, Jesus was always moved with love, grace, mercy, and compassion. Everyone, with the exception of the religious leaders, knew that if they could just touch His garment or get close enough, He was willing to save, heal, and deliver them.

Satan knew this as well; he tried his very best to hinder and deceive Jesus in the wilderness temptation. But it didn't go well for him, as although it may have been unfortunate for Satan, it was not unfortunate for humanity. Jesus resisted and defeated all of his temptations and lies. Shortly thereafter, the Lord wasted no time saving, healing, and delivering those who were in need. Matthew 4:17, 23 says, "From that time Jesus began to preach and to say, repent, for the kingdom of heaven is at hand ... And Jesus went about all Galilee, teaching in their synagogues, preaching the gospel of the kingdom, and healing all kinds of sickness and all kinds of disease among the people."

When speaking about the countless things we endure in life, many of us can agree that sickness and disease are at the top of the list. The Satanic kingdom is one of the primary causes of suffering in this world. Was Satan not the direct source of Job's suffering? Absolutely! (See Job 1:6–22.) And was he not the perpetrator who Jesus said inflicted a woman for eighteen years? Yes, indeed. (See

Luke 13:16.) It goes without saying that if sickness and disease are the direct results of satanic influence, then without reservation, many circumstances we encounter in life must be dealt with through the supernatural ministry of Christ.

Who is it that says the age of miracles, signs, and wonders has since passed away? Unfortunately, this is a lie that's being preached, written, and taught in many parts of the body of Christ. While on earth ministering salvation, healing, deliverance, and working miracles was a routine part of Christ ministry. The good news is that the Lord's ministry of saving, healing, deliverance, and miracles continues on. Jesus has sent the Holy Spirit (Helper, Advocate, Comforter, Administrator) to carry out heaven's agenda on earth.

> I have many things to say to you, but you are not able to bear them or to take them upon you or to grasp them now. But when He, the Spirit of truth (the Truth-giving Spirit) comes, He will guide you into all the Truth (the whole, full Truth). For He will not speak His own message [on His own authority]; but He will tell whatever He hears [from the Father; He will give the message that has been given to Him], and He will announce and declare to you the things that are to come [that will happen in the future]. He will honor and glorify Me, because He will take of (receive, draw upon) what is Mine and will reveal (declare, disclose, transmit) it to you. Everything that the Father has is Mine. That is what I meant when I said that He [the Spirit] will take the things that are Mine and will reveal (declare, disclose, transmit) it to you. (John 16:12–15 AMP)

My friend, it's a blessing to know that God has given us everything that pertains to life and godliness. The believer in Christ has been given spiritual resources to walk in victory. In addition, our most potent resource is communion with God through prayer. James 5:16

says, "The effective, fervent prayer of a righteous man avails much." Prayer is like a ballistic missile that can destroy an assigned target, for there's no time or distance in prayer. The Father hears the prayers of the righteous, and when we call on Him we're never disappointed. Psalm 145:18–19 says, "The Lord is near to all who call upon Him, to all who call upon Him in truth. He will fulfill the desire of those who fear Him; He also will hear their cry and save them."

Man is triune in nature and structure; he is spirit, soul, and body. (See 1 Thessalonians 5:23.) I shared this because many people, including Christians, are not fully aware the Lord is concerned about the total man and woman. It makes no difference what denominations or roles we have in the body of Christ; we're not exempt from depending on the Lord. That should encourage us, because as we walk with God, we'll encounter various types of circumstances, situations, problems, and needs. Remember: it was Paul who said, "We must through many tribulations enter the kingdom of God" (Acts 14:22).

Do you or your loved ones need healing or a miracle for a physical, emotional, or spiritual need? Could it be you have family issues or problems at your place of employment? Whatever the issue may be, Christ is able and willing to help. He's full of love and compassion. Psalm 145:8–9 says, "The Lord is gracious and full of compassion, slow to anger and great in mercy. The Lord is good to all, and His tender mercies are over all His works." It is my sincere heartfelt prayer that these devotionals, proclamations, and scriptures encourage, uplift, edify, comfort, and build your faith.

SECTION 1

✧✧✧

SCRIPTURES AND DEVOTIONS

Encouragement, Comfort, and Hope

COMPASSIONATE FATHER

In all their suffering He [God] also suffered,
and He personally rescued
them. In His love and mercy, He redeemed them. He lifted them
up and carried them through all the years.
—Isaiah 63:9

In the late eighties, while serving in the military, I was diagnosed with cancer, but the Lord graciously healed and delivered me. It wasn't until some years later that one of my relatives shared that when my father got news of my diagnosis, he cried deeply. After hearing this, I was greatly moved and knew he felt my pain and suffering. What's even more, I had never seen him cry, so the news of my circumstance must have really touched his heart. A parent's compassion for his or her suffering child makes the parent not only willing to get rid of or alleviate the child's pain but to suffer with the child as well. There is a strong bond and connection between them.

Similarly, when God's people were suffering, He felt their pain. Isaiah 63:9 says, "In all their suffering He [God] also suffered, and He personally rescued them." Our heavenly Father is compassionate toward our circumstances. The verb form "to have compassion" denotes a strong emotion. It carries the idea of "feeling with someone," sort of entering into his or her experience and sharing his or her pain or circumstances. People often use the expression "I feel you." What they're saying is "I understand and feel your pain." The heart of the Father's compassion is that He's willing to share in our human experience.

The story of the Good Samaritan is a great example of compassion.

1

He encountered a suffering man who needed help. What compelled his actions was compassion. (See Luke 10:33.) Sadly, there are not too many people similar to the Good Samaritan who will sympathize and have compassion toward your circumstance. But the good news is that Jesus is touched by our feelings and infirmities; He understands everything we're experiencing. Psalm 103:13 (NLT) says, "The Lord is like a father to His children, tender and compassionate to those who fear Him." Not only does the Father see and feel our circumstances, but He's also willing to do something about them.

✦✦✦

Be not dismayed whatever be tide, God will take care of you;
Beneath His wings of love abide, God will take care of you…
No matter what may be the test, God will take care of you,
Lean, weary one upon His breast, God will take care of you.[1]

 Further reading, meditation, and study—Isaiah 63:7–9; Luke 10:30–37

GOOD BEDSIDE MANNERISMS

The Lord God has given me the tongue of the learned,
that I should know how to speak a word in season to him
who is weary. He awakens Me morning by morning,
He awakens My ear, to hear as the learned.
—Isaiah 50:4

While there are physicians who genuinely care, there are doctors, surgeons, and medical specialists who have awful bedside manners. They make no effort to encourage, comfort, and connect with their patients. For instance, years ago I had developed a kidney stone. If you've ever had one—or more than one—you know how painful they can be. I experienced so much pain and discomfort that I was up all night literally tossing and rolling on the floor in our living room. The following day, my wife took me to the emergency room. We couldn't get there fast enough. Once we arrived at the emergency room, the doctor ordered a CAT scan. While we waited for my test results, I was experiencing excruciating pain.

There was a knock at the door; it was the doctor. There he stood. Never entering, with an unsympathetic, unemotional expression, he announced my results. "You have a kidney stone." My wife and I, from our previous conversation and interactions with him, concluded that he lacked good bedside manners. But I have good news for you. Jesus has good bedside mannerisms. We can come to Him for virtually everything, because He is touched by our infirmities. First Peter 5:7 says, "Casting all your care upon Him, for He cares for you."

God gave Christ the tongue of the learned that He should know how to speak a word in season to those who are weary. (See Isaiah 50:4.) When people are experiencing life's unexpected problems or enduring difficult circumstances, they need a word in season—a word of hope, comfort, and encouragement. It takes a mature man or woman of God with compassion and sympathy to speak a word of comfort to your need. Jesus is always available to those who need Him. We can take comfort in knowing that we can cast all of our cares on Him.

✦✦✦

 Further reading, meditation, and study—Isaiah 50:4–5; 2 Corinthians 1:3–7

FREEDOM FROM REJECTION

Having predestined us into the adoption
of children by Jesus Christ to
Himself, according to the good pleasure of His will,
to the praise of the glory of His grace, wherein
He hath made us accepted in the beloved.
—Ephesians 1:5–6

The spirit of rejection can produce three kinds of people: the person who gives in, the person who holds out, and the person who fights back. After many attempts of trying to fit in, those who have been rejected often eventually give in. They'll say things like, "I can't take this," "No one loves me," "No one cares," "I should just stay to myself," "I'd be better off dead," or "What's the use of living?" Many people are unaware that speaking unwholesome words can open the door for a barrage of negative situations, which may include rejection, loneliness, self-pity, misery, depression, despair, hopelessness, and suicide. (See Proverbs 18:21.)

Those people who refuse to give in build defensive barriers around themselves. They desperately try to appear happy, but deep down inside they're wounded by rejection. These are the Christians who shout and praise on Sunday morning but quickly sit down as though they've never experienced a move of the Spirit.

Finally, those people who fight everything and everybody often react with resentment and hatred. I witnessed this type of behavior many years ago. I ran into an old classmate who at times was the object of jokes. Back then it seemed there were always class comedians, and being an immature teenager, I often laughed at their jokes. I was glad to see this person, but as soon as I spoke, he looked at me with disgust and gave no response. Although forty years had elapsed, he had never moved past the jokes and laughter and had developed a spirit of rejection.

There are multitudes of people who find it difficult to move forward and fulfill their purpose because of rejection. It's worth mentioning that Jesus endured double rejection—rejection by both humans and the Father. First, He was rejected by humanity. (See Isaiah 53:3; John 1:12.) Second, during the last moments of the crucifixion, He experienced rejection from the Father. (See Matthew 27:45–46.) Jesus is the answer for those who suffer with rejection. He took our rejection so that we might experience His acceptance. (See Ephesians 1:6.) Because of the magnitude of betrayal, abandonment, and rejection, many feel it's beyond healing. But Jesus says He'll never leave you or forsake you. (See Hebrews 11:5.) And for every form of rejection, God has accepted us in the beloved (Jesus).

✧ ✧ ✧

 Further reading, meditation, and study—Isaiah 53:1–3; Ephesians 1:2–6

Staggering in Unbelief

He [Abraham] did not waver at the promise
of God through unbelief
but was strengthened in faith, giving glory to
God, and being fully convinced that
what He [God] had promised. He was able to perform.
—Romans 4:20–21

There are many churches and believers who make excuses for not believing and accepting certain things and promises in the Bible. What's more, many struggle to accept certain doctrines that our Lord Jesus and the apostles taught, such as supernatural gifts, healing, deliverance, casting out demons, speaking in tongues, and so on. So what could be the reason why so many reject or forfeit many of these precious promises and benefits in the Bible? I strongly believe that unbelief is the reason why some stagger at God's Word and His promises. It is not the promise or the Word of God that fails when we stagger, but our faith and trust in God.

Sadly, the outworking of a heart of unbelief cannot yield positive results. This is apparent in the New Testament. Even Jesus "did not do many mighty works there because of their unbelief" (Matthew 13:58). Just envision many sick and demon-possessed people who had had suffered for an extended period of time. Regrettably, they came around Christ not to resolve their issues, but to discredit His ministry. Unfortunately, because of unbelief many missed a valuable opportunity to be healed and delivered. Today we pray and believe by faith for our breakthroughs, but for the people of Jesus's time, He was right in front of them.

As a result of the atoning work of Christ, we have a better covenant established on better promises. Hebrews 8:6 (AMP) says, "But as it now is, He [Christ] has acquired a [priestly] ministry which is as much superior and more excellent [than the old] as the covenant (the agreement) of which He is the Mediator (the Arbiter, Agent) is superior and more excellent, [because] it is enacted and rests upon more important (sublimer, higher, and nobler) promises." God does not want His children lacking and forfeiting precious promises, because of what Christ did at the cross. But again, it's not the promise or the Word of God that fails when we stagger in unbelief, but our faith and trust in God.

✦ ✦ ✦

   Further reading, meditation, and study—Matthew 13:53–58; Romans 4:13–20

HUMANKIND'S INABILITY; GOD'S OPPORTUNITY

Ah, Lord God! Behold, You have made the heavens and the
earth by Your great power and outstretched arm. There is
nothing too hard for You … Behold, I am
the Lord, the God of all flesh.
Is there anything too hard for Me?
—Jeremiah 32:17, 27

Jesus's discourse with a rich young ruler who wasn't ready to commit and depart with his riches prompted an important question from those who stood by: "Who then can be saved?" (Luke 18:26). Jesus immediately responded with a statement I believe encompasses not only salvation but everything we cannot accomplish or attain ourselves. Jesus said, "The things which are impossible with men are possible with God" (v. 27). For those who feel there's no hope or likelihood their circumstance will ever change, that has to be an encouraging word. Man's inability is God's opportunity.

Consider Abraham and Sarah in the Old Testament. As a result of the aging of their bodies, they were unable to have children. However, instead of Abraham focusing on their physical inadequacies, he was "fully convinced that what He [God] had promised He was also able to perform" (Romans 4:21). God is omnipotent and specializes in the impossible. Oh, how we at times forget we serve a powerful God. The Bible says, "God has spoken once, twice I have heard this; that power belongs to God" (Psalm 62:11).

Maybe you know someone who recently received a negative medical prognosis, who had a bank loan denied based on credit history, or something similar. When our backs are against the wall, we must recall what Jesus said: "The things which are impossible with men [doctors, medical specialists, loan officers, and such] are possible with God" (Luke 18:27). Confessing God's Word over our lives for the devil to hear it is also important. Why? Because "they overcame him [devil] by the blood of the lamb and by the word of their testimony, and they did not love their lives to death" (Revelation 12:11). So no matter what our circumstances look like from a natural or human standpoint, we must believe that with God all things are possible.

❖ ❖ ❖

The giants that are in front of you are
never bigger than the God who lives in you!

  Further reading, meditation, and study—Jeremiah 32:16–27; Luke 18:24–27

SIMPLY BELIEVE

For with God nothing will be impossible. Then Mary said behold the maidservant of the Lord! Let it be to me according to your word and the angel departed from her.
—Luke 1:37–38

A very good quality that many men and women demonstrated in the Bible was their willingness to believe and apply God's Word to their circumstances. They knew the prerequisite for receiving from the Lord was to simply believe. Their refusal to walk in unbelief moved the Lord to deliver on His promises, and they were often commended. My friend, nothing has changed as it pertains to receiving from the Lord. Faith is a major prerequisite for receiving from Him. Matthew 15:28 says, "Then Jesus answered and said to her, O woman great is your faith! Let it be to you as you desire. And her daughter was healed from that very hour."

For instance, Mary received an important promise and revelation about becoming the mother of Jesus. Consider the implication of that promise. On earth she would be the mother of the Son of God. She would have a pivotal role in bringing in the greatest and most powerful human in the universe. According to Luke 1:32, the Bible says, Jesus "Will be great, and will be called the Son of the Highest; and the Lord God will give Him the throne of His father David." I suspect Mary wasn't prepared for such an overwhelming blessing. But how she responded gives us a pattern of how we should respond to the promises of God.

Luke 1:38 says, "Then Mary said, Behold the maidservant of the Lord! Let it be to me according to your word. And the angel departed

11

from her." Mary heard what the angel declared, and it moved her to say in faith, "Let it be according to your word." To put it another way, Mary was saying that if God spoke it, it was as good as done. Similarly to many of the patriots in the Bible, she knew that "God is not a man, that He should lie" (Numbers 23:19). Whatever the Bible says about us and our circumstances, we must believe and take God at His word.

✧✧✧

Through it all, through it all, I've learned to trust in Jesus
I've learned to trust in God; Through it all, through it all
I've learned to depend upon His Word.[2]

 Further reading, meditation, and study—Luke 1:26–38; Acts 27:13–38

ALWAYS ON TIME

Therefore, the sisters [Mary, Martha] sent
to Him, saying, Lord, behold
he [Lazarus] whom You love is sick. When
Jesus heard that, He said, this sickness
is not unto death but for the glory of God that the Son of God
may be glorified through it.
—John 11:3–4

Jesus had full knowledge of Lazarus's condition, but it wasn't until four days later that He arrived at His friend's home. By that time, people were emotionally distressed, and both sisters had to be comforted. Martha said, "If You had been here, my brother would not have died" (v. 21). It appears they either forgot or struggled to believe what Jesus said earlier: "This sickness is not unto death, but for the glory of God" (v. 4). Before many of us rush to any conclusions, we too, at times, soon forget what God promises through His Word. In all fairness, it must have been a difficult time for the entire family, considering the surrounding circumstances.

Similarly, there are times when we allow things to eclipse our trust and dismantle our faith. We approach life's problems as though the Lord is not in sight and nowhere to be found. To put it another way, we approach many things through the lenses of unbelief. If only we could ask the woman who had an issue of blood for twelve years what was going on in her mind during those trying times. Or if we could ask the woman with a spirit of infirmity for eighteen years how she managed to get around. How about the man with an infirmity for thirty-eight years? What kept him from giving up?

Perhaps they would say, "He may not come when we want Him or answer us right away when we pray, but He's always on time." If you read their stories, you'll find they had at least one thing in common. The answers to their circumstances were delayed but never denied. When the answers to our problems seem like they're delayed, we can take comfort that "All things work together for good to those who love God, to those who are the called according to His purpose" (Romans 8:28). We can be confident that God is behind the scenes, putting things in order. The trial was allowed not so it would damage or destroy us, but for the glory of God.

✦ ✦ ✦

Those who leave everything in God's hand will
eventually see God's hand in everything.

 Further reading, meditation, and study—Mark 5:21–43; John 11:1–44

THE WAY, TRUTH, AND DOOR

Then Jesus said to them again, most assuredly,
I say to you, I am the door
of the sheep. All who ever came before Me are
thieves and robbers, but the sheep did
not hear them ... Jesus said to him, I am the
way, the truth, and the life. No one
comes to the Father except through Me.
—John 10:7; 14:6

The Bible is very clear concerning the way to the Father and the plan of salvation, (Jesus Himself said that [He is] the way, truth, and the life. No one comes to the Father except through [Him]." (see John 14:6). This is one of those scriptures that ruffles the feathers of many religious groups. If you want to know where people stand as it relates to God's plan of salvation, start a discussion with this scripture and you'll cut to the chase. They'll wholeheartedly agree with you or argue with you. Jesus is the way, truth, and the life. He paid an incredible price at Calvary; we must never compromise our position on that truth.

A couple of chapters prior to Jesus making this declaration, He says something that puts to rest the rationale that there are many ways to God. John 10:7 says, "I say to you I am the door of the sheep, all who ever came before Me are thieves and robbers ..." There is only one way to the Father, for Jesus Himself said He is the way, the door, and He also said that we are to enter through the narrow gate. (See Matthew 7:13–14; John 10:7, 14:6.) There are many who go in by the wide gate and broad way. This lets us know that doing so is a conscious decision on one's part. We'll either choose the narrow gate, which is the way of salvation, or the wide gate, which is the way of the world.

The atoning work of Jesus has made provision for salvation. The Lord will never twist our arm or place us at gunpoint, so to speak, to receive Him. He has given us free will to make a decision to choose either eternal life or eternal death. Romans 8:9 says, "That if you confess with your mouth the Lord Jesus and believe in your heart that God has raised Him from the dead, you will be saved." What a beautiful promise given to those who receive Jesus; there's no more uncertainty regarding the future. It is a blessing knowing that when Jesus becomes Lord and Savior of our lives, we have received the complete gift of salvation.

✧ ✧ ✧

Lord God, thank You for sending Your son Jesus to die for me. I know that without him I would be separated from You forever. I repent of my all my sins, and I invite You, Jesus, into my life as my personal Lord and Savior. Lord Jesus, baptize me with the Holy Spirit so that I can live for You. Lord, help me find a true body of believers, that I may grow in grace. Now take full control of my life in the name of Jesus. Amen!

 Further reading, meditation, and study—John 10:1–21; John 14:1–6; Acts 4:5–12

UNWAVERING TRUST

*This poor man cried out, and the Lord heard him, and saved him
out of all his troubles ... Oh, taste and see
that the Lord is good; blessed is
the man who trusts in Him [God]!*
—Psalm 34:6, 8

There are multitudes of people who believe that trusting the Lord can be very difficult. Not only does God want us to trust Him; he wants us to do so without wavering. To waver means to be indecisive, stagger, think twice, and hesitate. God's desire is that we simply believe and trust Him at His Word. This is a challenge for many people. For the record, I have nothing against medical doctors, specialists, and surgeons. We're all grateful for their fields of expertise; they're a wonderful benefit to society and the medical industry. But even with all the good they bring to our society, we're warned in the Bible that "It is better to trust in the Lord, than to put confidence in man" (Psalm 118:8).

What's even more, we're encouraged to "Lift up [our] eyes to the hills, from whence comes [our] help? [our] help comes from the Lord, who made heaven and earth" (Psalm 121:1–2, emphasis added). However, in the Old Testament, there was a king named Asa who had a severe disease in his feet and who chose not to seek the Lord, but only physicians. Accordingly, he placed all his trust in the arm of flesh instead of trusting God to heal him. Unfortunately for Asa, things didn't go as expected. Had he sought the Lord, he would not have died prematurely. (See 2 Chronicles 16:12–13.)

Likewise, many in this life are faced with overwhelming

17

circumstances and hardships that are hard to bear and beyond their control. But instead of seeking the Lord's healing and deliverance, many turn to humankind. However, we're told in the Bible, "Trust the Lord with all your heart, and lean not on your own understanding, in all your ways acknowledge [recognize] Him [God] … It will be health to your flesh, and strength to your bones" (Proverbs 3:5, 8). Acknowledging God first gives Him the opportunity to act on our behalf—something He's compassionate about and willingly wants to do.

❖ ❖ ❖

People are limited; they can offer only so much help.
On the other hand, God is unlimited in His capacity to help.
Humankind's inability is God's opportunity.

 Further reading, meditation, and study—Psalm 118:1–9; Proverbs 3:1–5; Nahum 1:7

FULLY CONVINCED

Who, contrary to hope, in hope believed,
so that He [Abraham] became the
father of many nations, according to what was
spoken, so shall your descendants be…
And being fully convinced that what He [God] had promised
He was also able to perform.
—Romans 4:18, 21

From a human perspective, Abraham received a promise from God, that seemed virtually impossible to believe. Taking into account his old age combined with the deadness of Sarah's womb, it seems it would take a miracle for the promise to come into fruition. Abraham's life was marked by all kinds of obstacles, hindrances, and tests. However, in spite of his circumstances, he believed God. (See Romans 4:18, 21.) In His book "The Ten Laws of Lasting Love," Paul Pearsall describes an important episode in a battle he faced against cancer.

> Any time a doctor came with news of my progress, my wife would join with me in a mutual embrace. The reports were seldom good during the early phases of my illness, and one day a doctor brought particularly frightening news. Gazing at his clipboard, he murmured, it doesn't look like you're going to make it. Before I could ask a question of this doomsayer, my wife stood up, handed me my robe, adjusted the tubes attached to my body and said, let's get out of

here. This man is a risk to your health. As she helped me struggle to the door, the doctor approached us, stay back, demanded my wife, stay away from us. As we walked together down the hall, the doctor attempted to catch up with us, keep going, said my wife, pushing the intravenous stand.

We're going to talk to someone who really knows what is going on. Then she held up her hand to the doctor, don't come any closer to us. The two of us moved as one. We fled to the safety and hope of a doctor who did not confuse diagnosis with verdict. I could never have made that walk toward wellness alone.[3]

What an encouraging testimony to help build and strengthen our faith. Whatever our circumstances are, we must not allow our senses or doctors to prevent us from releasing our faith to believe and receive from the Lord.

    Further reading, meditation, and study—Romans 4:13–25; Hebrews 4:14–16; 6:13–18

GILGAL A PLACE OF TRUST

Then the manna ceased on the day after
they had eaten the produce
of the land; and the children of Israel no
longer had manna, but they ate the
food of the land of Canaan that year.
—Joshua 5:12

As soon as the Israelites reached Gilgal, they had to transition from getting everything they needed to exercising faith and trust in God. When they came out of Egypt, God sustained them in every way. At one point, God reminded them of His provision: "You have seen what I did to the Egyptians, and how I bore [sustained] you on eagles' wings and brought you to Myself" (Exodus 19:4). Furthermore, God led them by a cloud by day and a pillar of fire by night. When they needed food and drink, that was no problem; the Lord allowed them to awaken every day to fresh manna from heaven. When they wanted meat, that was no problem; He provided quail in abundance. But when they arrived at Gilgal, the free gifts ceased, and faith had to be activated.

Early in our walk with God, it wasn't uncommon to pray and to receive immediate answers for something or someone else's needs. It seemed as though there were short waiting periods. Some time ago, my wife said that when she first got saved her prayers were answered right away. But as she grew in the Lord, it seemed they were delayed. This made me think of a time I heard a preacher give an illustration about the Lord and three Christians. He said that when the Lord approached the first new convert, He wrapped His arms around him.

The Lord then passed by the second Christian, who had grown in his faith, and gently patted his head. This Christian didn't need as much affirmation and encouragement. And finally, the Lord simply passed by and nodded at the third Christian. This individual had matured to a place where he could trust God in the process. He didn't need a lot of hugs and pats; he was able to stand on his own two feet and trust God. I believe this is what God was doing with the Israelites—bringing them to a place where they could trust and rely on Him completely. Psalm 37:3 (AMP) says, "Trust (lean on, rely on, and be confident) in the Lord and do good; so shall you dwell in the land and feed surely on His faithfulness, and truly you shall be fed." We must never fret when things don't come to us as quickly as we would like; we must trust God and wait patiently for Him.

✧ ✧ ✧

 Further reading, meditation, and study—Joshua 5:10–12; Psalm 37:3–6

JEHOVAH-RAPHA

He also brought them out with silver and gold, and there was none
feeble among His tribes. Egypt was glad
when they departed, for the fear of
them had fallen upon them. He spread a cloud for a covering, and
fire to give light in the night.
—Psalm 105:37–38

Unfortunately, there are many critics, doubters, naysayers, and those
who oppose divine healing, but the Lord has not changed His mind
since the Old Testament concerning complete health for all of His
children. It has always been His divine will for His children to walk
in wholeness. When the Israelites came out of Egypt, God's hand
was heavy upon them in every way. Psalm 10:37 says, "He [God]
also brought them out with silver and gold, and there was none
feeble among them." One of the most important names for God is
"Yahweh" or "Jehovah," from the verb "to be," meaning simply
"He is."

The redemptive name "Jehovah-Rapha" is translated as "I am the
Lord your Physician" or "I am the Lord that healeth thee" (Exodus
15:26). Not only did God heal the Israelites of sickness and disease,
but He made them prosperous too. I strongly believe Christ wants us
to experience complete health and prosperity as well. Since God is
not a respecter of persons, what He did for the Israelites as it relates
to healing, I believe, is His desire for His children today. Third John
2 says, "Beloved I pray that you may prosper in all things and be in
health, just as your soul prospers."

After the Israelites were liberated from Egypt, God promised He would remain their healer. It wasn't a one-time event of deliverance and healing. It would continue as long as they heeded His voice. Exodus 23:25–26 (NIV) says, "Worship the Lord your God, and His blessing will be on your food and water. I will take away sickness from among you, and none will miscarry or be barren in your land. I will give you a full life span." Similarly, as long as we heed or obey the voice of God and embrace the many benefits and promises of the Bible, they can become ours as well.

❖ ❖ ❖

 Further reading, meditation, and study—Exodus 15:22–27; Matthew 8:1–17

FRUITFUL AND AFFLICTED

And the name of the second he called Ephraim; for God has
caused me [Joseph] to be fruitful in the land of my affliction.
—Genesis 41:52

When Joseph's father, Jacob, was a young adolescent, his mother
favored him, while his father favored his twin, Esau. This offended
his brothers and nearly destroyed their family. This generational
curse continued on later, because Jacob practiced the same kind of
favoritism toward his twelve children. This, of course, provoked
conflict among the siblings and created a hostile environment for
Joseph. Things got bad when Jacob made a colorful ornamented coat,
a show of preference and favoritism that made Joseph's brothers angry
and jealous toward him.

Things seemed to worsen and were aggravated when the Lord
showed Joseph a series of dreams that indicated he would one day lead
his family. Joseph shared his dreams with his family, and this upset
his older brothers. They became envious of him, and even his father
was concerned but kept the matter in mind. (See Genesis 37:11.) To
make a long story short, Joseph's brothers saw an opportunity to vent
their jealousy by first placing Joseph in a pit and then selling him
to traders. He ended up in Egypt, wrongfully accused by Potiphar's
wife, and was thrown in prison for fourteen years.

Some years later, Pharaoh had a dream. Joseph interpreted his
dream and was let out and made second in charge in all of Egypt.
Later on, he had a family, and he named one of his sons Ephraim,
which literally means "fruitfulness." Joseph said, "For God has caused
me to be fruitful in the land of my affliction" (Genesis 41:52). I took

25

time to share his account because many of us can certainly identify with Joseph to some degree. I have come to realize it makes no difference where God plants us or what we may experience in this life. We serve a powerful God who is able and willing to make us fruitful in the land of our afflictions.

✧ ✧ ✧

 Further reading, meditation, and study—Genesis 41:37–57; Romans 8:28

TOUCHED HIM

...And besought Him [Christ] that they might only touch the hem
of His garment; and as many as touched
it were made perfectly whole.
—Matthew 14:36 (KJV)

Much can be said about those who stood far off and those who pressed in to touch Christ. It's important to note that not all among the crowds that thronged Him received healing, but as many as touched Him were made perfectly whole. This gives us the understanding that we must be resolute in receiving our miracles, healing, deliverance, or breakthroughs. We're encouraged to "Come boldly to the throne of grace, that we may obtain mercy and find grace to help in time of need" (Hebrews 4:16).

The woman with the issue of blood, along with so many others in the Bible, is an example of faith and determination. But can you imagine a massive crowd in one place? Yet this is what the woman with the issue of blood had to press through to touch Jesus. Perhaps she may have been anemic, considering her twelve-year bout with an issue of blood. If your body loses blood, it will become weak and feeble. Envision this weak and feeble woman having to push through a crowd of people. Yet she was persistent and determined to touch Jesus.

What a contrast there is between those in the crowd who were only curious about Christ and this woman who reached out and touched Him. When there's a problem or illness that demands the Master's touch, we must press clear of the traditions of men, unbelief, public opinion, complacency, and lukewarmness. What's even more, you might have to press beyond your spiritual leader's or pastor's theology if it does not line up with God's Word. Receiving your healing and breakthrough is more important than the opinions of people. By faith we must touch the Lord without reservation and with a determination to receive from Him.

✦ ✦ ✦

 Further reading, meditation, and study—Matthew 14:34–36; Luke 8:40–48

Yoke of Bondage

Stand fast therefore in the liberty by which
Christ has made us free, and
do not be entangled again with a yoke of
bondage … You have become estranged
from Christ, you who attempt to be justified
by law; you have fallen from grace.
—Galatians 5:1, 4

If there were two opposites in the Bible, they would be the Mosaic law and grace. They were given at different dispensations. John 1:17 says, "For the Law was given through Moses, but grace and truth came through Jesus Christ." A simple distinction between law and grace would be this: The law would say, "This is what you have to do and keep all the time," while grace would say, "Someone else has done it for you." That someone is none other than Jesus Christ. Hebrews 8:6 says, "He [Christ] has obtained a more excellent ministry, inasmuch as He is also Mediator of a better covenant, which was established on better promises."

Unfortunately, there are multitudes of well-meaning Christians who are unclear in their understanding of the difference between law and grace. So, with an incomplete revelation, no sound teaching, and no understanding, they try to mix the two together. As a result, they struggle to live the kind of life God wants them to have or to enjoy the salvation that's been promised through Jesus. This leaves many struggling to demonstrate joy and peace, and they are very cynical, critical, and judgmental. I believe you would agree that some of the unkindest and most unpleasant people in the body of Christ are those bound by legalism.

There are many who find themselves in some form of spiritual bondage, always reverting back to human-made rules and the traditions of people. The Lord Jesus can unshackle them and set them free. He delivers people from sin but also liberates people from the bondage of legalism. (See John 8:31–32.) So we're told to "stand fast therefore in the liberty by which Christ has made us free, and do not be entangled again with a yoke of bondage" (Galatians 5:1). If you would like to know more about being set free from legalism or religious tradition, please get my book entitled *Freedom from Spiritual Bondage*: Breaking Free from Religious Tradition and Legalism, Surrendering to the Holy Spirit, and Embracing Sonship and Grace.

 Further reading, meditation, and study—Matthew 11:28–30; Galatians 3:1–3; 4:21–31; 5:1–6

INCREDIBLE MEMORY

> God heard their groaning and He remembered His covenant
> with Abraham with Isaac and with Jacob.
> So God looked on the Israelites
> and was concerned about them.
> —Exodus 2:24–25 (NIV)

Often during times of testing or in the midst of circumstances, the devil will speak lies into our ears, speaking falsely about God's faithfulness and trying to discredit His promises to us. He'll even make you feel like there's no hope. He will say things like, "Look at you now; the Lord hasn't healed you, the Lord hasn't delivered you, the Lord hasn't made good on His promise to you, and He has probably forgotten you." We must always remember that everything the devil says is a lie. Jesus said, "There is no truth in him. When he speaks a lie, he speaks from his own resources, for he is a liar and the father of it" (John 8:44).

It always puts a smile upon my face and blesses me when I read in the Bible phrases like "God remembered His covenant" or "God remembered." When we see these types of promises in the Bible, it should give us confidence and comfort knowing that our Heavenly Father does not have spiritual amnesia. No matter how much time has elapsed, He still remembers the promise He made to us as though it were yesterday or a minute ago. In the Old Testament, Noah was in the ark for an extended period, but "God remembered Noah" (Genesis 8:1).

It makes no difference how long you've been battling or struggling under the weight of your circumstances. God has incredible memory.

31

Unlike we humans, He doesn't have memory lapses. God has not forgotten you. Perhaps you're sick or in the hospital and have been there for quite some time. God has not forgotten you. Maybe you're presently in the nursing home and have no family and no one seems to care or come to visit you. God hasn't forgotten you. Always remember that God will deliver and make good on whatever promise He made to you.

✧✧✧

 Further reading, meditation, and study—Genesis 8:1–19; Exodus 2:23–25

COMPASSIONATE CHRIST

The Lord is gracious and full of compassion, slow to anger
and great in mercy. The Lord is good to all, and His tender
mercies are over all His works.
—Psalm 145:8–9

In Biblical times, when the sick sought healing they would ask for God's mercy. In the Bible, "mercy" and "compassion" have the same meaning. The Hebrew noun "*rachamin*" is translated both as "mercy" and "compassion." The Greek verb "*eleeo*" is translated as "have mercy and have compassion." When we take into account Christ as healer, we must bear in mind that He was abundant in mercy and full of compassion. Although He was the most powerful person who ever walked this earth, He exercised His immense power to assist and relieve human needs from a compassionate heart.

Taking into account the Lord's compassion, we have a complete revelation of His willingness to heal. By always healing the sick, Christ unveiled the compassionate heart of God to the people. Satan has always worked hard to hide this glorious fact, and sadly many people have bought into his lies. He has echoed the words of many who say that the age of miracles is past gone and not for us today. What they have failed to understand and appreciate is that Jesus's compassionate heart toward human needs hasn't changed. "Jesus Christ (the Messiah) is [always] the same, yesterday, today, [yes] and forever (to the ages)" (Hebrews 13:8 AMP).

Jesus warned us that the devil is a liar and the father of it. (See John 8:44.) So no matter what you're experiencing, no matter what the physicians and surgeons have told you, and no matter what some preachers have said against it, the Lord still heals and works miracles today. You and I can have full assurance and expectation that He's able and willing to heal and deliver us and our loved ones. We have assurance knowing that Jesus is seated at the right hand of the Father, making intercession for us.

✧✧✧

 Further reading, meditation, and study—Psalm 145:1–9; Luke 10:30–37

HAGAR AND SARAH

... For it is written that Abraham had two sons;
the one by a bondwoman [Hagar] the
other by a freewoman [Sarah]. But he who was of the
bondwoman was born according to the flesh, and he of he
freewoman through promise... So then, brethren we are not
children of the bondwoman but of the free.
—Galatians 4:21–23, 31

Hagar and Sarah represent two types of covenants. Hagar was Abraham's and Sarah's bondwoman, a slave who bore Ishmael, who was not of the promise. Hagar represents the old covenant under the Mosaic law, and Sarah represents the new covenant under Christ, also known as the New Testament. Sarah was barren, and it seemed as though God had not given her favor, as opposed to Hagar, her bondwoman. But in due time, God visited Sarah. At God's appointed time, she was more blessed than her bondwoman. Likewise, Judaism, the legalistic and religious system during Jesus's time, was very aggressive.

At the appointed time, Jesus appeared, being full of grace and truth. Judaism, being somewhat of the legalistic system of that day, had many in bondage, but it lost its power and weakened. It had always been God's good intention to form a new covenant with His people. He had promised this in Jeremiah 31:31: "Behold the days are coming says the Lord when I will make a new covenant with the house of Israel and with the house of Judah." Apparently this covenant was given to His chosen people, but it also includes those who are Gentiles and have been grafted in because of the atonement of Christ. (See Isaiah 56:8; John 10:16.)

The good news is that we're under a "more excellent ministry ... inasmuch as He [Jesus] is also mediator of a better covenant which was established on better promises" (Hebrews 8:6). But there seems to be one major problem: many of God's precious people have not fully embraced the new covenant and are still living under the old covenant of laws and rules (legalism). The thing we should bear in mind is that once we have received Christ, we're now partakers of God's divine grace. We willingly look to Christ alone for justification and salvation. We do not rely on laws and rules as means of serving and living for the Lord.

📖 Further reading, meditation, and study—Galatians 4:21–31; Hebrews 8:1–13

No Partiality

Then Peter opened his mouth and said; in truth I perceive that
God shows no partiality. But in every nation
whoever fears Him and works
righteousness is accepted by Him.
—Acts 10:34–35

Christ never turned anyone away who believed He was able and willing to heal and deliver them. This is very important for us to grasp, especially for those who are battling some type of sickness or disease. Although many of us have read case studies and testimonies in the Bible about Christ healing and delivering people, there are some who have bought into the lie that their circumstances don't meet His criteria or that Christ doesn't heal today. Personally, I find this sad and alarming, because never was there a moment in Scripture or life when Christ ignored, sidestepped, and overlooked the pain and suffering of humankind.

Consider the ten lepers in the New Testament, who were located in the region of Samaria and Galilee. (See Luke 17:11–15.) During Biblical times, leprosy was a slow, progressive, and incurable chronic skin disease. It was characterized by sores, scabs, and shining white spots beneath the skin. What's more, if the symptoms of leprosy showed up in a person, the law required that the person be isolated or quarantined from the rest of society. (See Leviticus 13:45–46.) Furthermore, if anyone made contact with the disease, he or she was considered defiled.

Throughout the Scriptures, it is evident that our Lord Jesus was moved by love and compassion, seeing as He often disregarded any narrative about leprosy or any other type of disease. Although the lepers stood at a distance when they encountered Jesus, He still ministered to their needs. He told them, "Go, show yourselves to the priests, and so it was that as they went, they were cleansed" (Luke 17:14). It's encouraging to know that our Lord Jesus will meet us at our point of need, no matter what we have or struggle with. He's no respecter of persons.

✧ ✧ ✧

 Further reading, meditation, and study—Matt. 9:35–37; Luke 17:11–19; Luke 19:1–10

ABLE AND WILLING

Now when Jesus had entered Capernaum,
a centurion came to Him
pleading with Him, saying, Lord my servant
is lying home paralyzed dreadfully
tormented. And Jesus said to him, I will come and heal him.
—Matthew 8:5–7

There is vast difference between the words "able" and "willing." For instance, I might say you're able to help me, but that doesn't mean you will; it means only that you're capable of helping me. You may even have all the necessary tools and means to alleviate my problem but still fail to do so. However, Jesus is always willing to assist in the needs of humankind. Throughout the New Testament, we see Biblical case studies and examples of people who called out to Jesus, and Jesus always stopped to assist. Never was there a moment when He did not respond to those whose faith grabbed hold of Him.

Consider the Centurion that asked Jesus to come and heal his servant. Matthew 8:5–7 says, "Now when Jesus had entered Capernaum, a Centurion came to Him, pleading with Him, saying Lord my servant is lying at home paralyzed, dreadfully tormented. And Jesus said to him, I will come and heal him." Jesus responds, "I will come and heal him." But please note that Jesus does not say, "I'm able to heal him," but instead leaves him hanging and without help. He responds by saying, "I will come and heal him."

My friend, it's makes no difference what challenges you're facing, whether they be financial matters, health issues, relationship problems, employment issues, or so on. Not only is Jesus able, but

He's willing to meet you at your point of need. Hebrews 4:16 (AMP) says, "Let us then fearlessly and confidently and boldly draw near to the throne of grace (the throne of God's unmerited favor to us, sinners), that we may receive mercy [for our failures] and find grace to help in good time for every need [appropriate help and well-timed help, coming just when we need it]." This scripture covers everything; there's nothing impossible with God.

He is Jehovah, God of creation. He is Jehovah
Lord God almighty, the Balm of Gilead, the Rock of Ages,
He is Jehovah, the God that healeth thee.[4]

    Further reading, meditation, and study—Matthew 8:1–13; Luke 8:40–56

PERSISTENCE

Then He spoke a parable to them, that men always ought to pray and not lose hear ... Be sober, be vigilant your adversary the devil walks about like a roaring lion, seeking whom he may devour. Resist him, steadfast in the faith ...
—Luke 18:1; 1 Peter 5:8–9

Persistence is one of Satan's primary weapons of attack. He doesn't relent until he gains victory over his victims. Peter warns us that "the devil walks about like a roaring lion, seeking whom he may devour" (1 Peter 5:8). I read a story about a man that was once a part of Satan's camp; he wrote how he was taught to be persistent when using evil powers. He went on to say that doing so would weaken his opponent and interrupt their fight. Many Christians haven't given much thought to this type of demonic strategy. Consider Satan's defeat in the wilderness and his persistence going forth. Luke 4:13 says, "Now when the devil had ended every temptation, he departed from Him [Jesus] until an opportune time."

Notice again how "the [devil] departed from Him [Jesus] until an opportune time." The word "opportune" means "favorable," "right," "suitable," "convenient," and "well-timed." The devil was defeated in the wilderness, but he waited for a favorable, right, suitable, convenient time to strike Jesus again, but to no avail. Another example of Satan's persistence is the account of Paul confronting a girl possessed with a spirit of divination. (See Acts 16:16–18.) Satan's persistence was a strategic one; it was an attempt to entrap the people after Paul and Silas left the region. If Paul hadn't counterattacked by casting out the demon, the people would have believed the slave girl, and she would have continued her witchcraft.

The parable of the widow in Luke 18 is an example of how believers must be persistent against our adversary the devil. The word "adversary" means "opponent," "enemy," "foe," and "antagonist." Peter describes Satan as an adversary as well. (See 1 Peter 5:8.) The widow was resolute in getting justice from her adversary. Nothing could stop her determination and persistence. That is how we must counteract the devil's attacks. Jesus said that "men always ought to pray and not lose heart" (Luke 18:1). Through the power of the Spirit and effectual, fervent praying, we can overcome every persistent attack from the devil.

 Further reading, meditation, and study—Mark 10:46–52; Luke 18:1–8

Manufacturer's Warranty

For You formed my inward parts; You
covered me in my mother's womb.
I will praise You, for I am fearfully and wonderfully
made; marvelous are Your works, and that
my soul knows very well. My frame was not hidden
from You, when I was made in secret
and skillfully wrought in the lowest parts of the earth.
—Psalm 139:13–14

You can clearly see from reading the above scripture that God took great care and was very intentional in how He formed us in our mothers' wombs. What a blessing to know that our Heavenly Father took time to mold and shape us. In other words, we were not created by chance or accidents waiting to happen; we were fearfully and wonderfully made. Every part of our physical frames was made with extreme caution, care, and love by the Lord. Consider this: Every human in the world has a distinct personality and unique appearance. What's more, everyone has a set of fingerprints that are not the same, and the same goes for our DNA.

You may or may not agree with what I am about to say next, but I believe our physical frames have lifetime warranties on all external and internal parts. The Lord, our Manufacturer, knows everything about us; even the hairs on our heads are numbered. What's more, Job, in the midst of suffering, knew God's hands had made him and fashioned him, for he declared how God "Clothed him with skin and flesh, and knit him together with bones and sinews" (Job 10:8–11). I believe Job was implying that if God clothed my skin and flesh, and knit my bones and tendons, He's able to heal and deliver me from any affliction.

Consider an automobile, or some type of engine, with a malfunction. Depending on the type of warranty that came with it, the manufacturer will either fix or replace the malfunctioning parts. Similarly, when we're faced with circumstances, or when sickness and disease attack our physical bodies, our Spiritual Manufacturer (God) is able and willing to heal and deliver us if we cry out to Him in faith. (See Matthew 7:7–8.) We must claim the promises of the Bible (our spiritual manufacturer's warranty) so that God (our Spiritual Manufacturer) can heal us, deliver us, or give us a creative miracle if need be.

📖 Further reading, meditation, and study—Psalm 139:13–15; Matthew 8:1–17

FAITH, NOT SIGHT

For we walk by faith [we regulate our lives
and conduct ourselves by our
conviction or belief respecting man's relationship
to God and divine things, with trust and
holy fervor, this we walk] not by sight or appearance.
—2 Corinthians 5:7 (AMP)

True Biblical faith is based not on evidence of our physical senses but on the eternal, invisible truths revealed by God's Word. Most Christians approach life, spiritual things, and circumstances from a positive perspective; they're not guided by what their senses reveal but walk by faith and not by sight. (See 2 Corinthians 5:7.) Notice that faith is contrasted with sight. Sight, along with our other physical senses, is related to the objects of the physical world. But faith is connected to truths revealed in God's Word. Additionally, our senses deal with things that are material, temporal, and changeable, but faith is related to things that are invisible, eternal, and unchanging.

There are two types of Christians: those who are carnally minded and those who are spiritually minded. Carnally minded Christians do not approach biblical principles from an origination of faith. They accept what their senses reveal. With them, everything, including the Bible, is considered and looked at from a natural and logical standpoint instead of a spiritual one. (See 2 Corinthians 2:14.) The truth of God's Word is more real to the spiritually minded than what their senses reveal to them. They base their faith on God's Word, not what they experience or their senses reveal to them. Romans 4:19–21 says, "And not being weak in faith, he did not consider his

45

own body, already dead since he was about a hundred years old, and the deadness of Sarah's womb."

Abraham refused to accept the testimony of his senses. His senses indicated that he and Sarah were no longer able to have children. But Abraham's faith would not allow this testimony, because it did not agree with what God said. His faith was aligned with promise (the substance of things hoped for). Likewise, you and I have to take this same approach. Whatever God's Word declares, we must allow our mouths to come into agreement with it. If, for whatever reason, we struggle to believe, we should feed our faith and starve our unbelief. So let's focus more on God's Word than on what our senses reveal.

✧ ✧ ✧

 Further reading, meditation, and study—Romans 4:13–22; Hebrews 11:1–40

COMPASSION AND SYMPATHY

When Jesus heard it, He departed from there
by boat to a deserted place by
Himself. But when the multitudes heard it, they
followed Him on foot from the cities.
And when Jesus went out He saw a great
multitude; and He was moved
with compassion for them, and healed their sick.
—Matthew 14:13–14

Compassion and sympathy were some of the cornerstones in Jesus's ministry while He was on earth, and they still are. We receive this wonderful ministry from Him because He's seated at the right hand of the Father, making intercession for us. Jesus always demonstrated love, compassion and sympathy to those He came in contact with. Likewise, compassion and sympathy should always be evident in every ministry and among God's people. First Peter 3:8 says, "Finally all of you, live in harmony with one another; be sympathetic, love as brothers, be compassionate and humble."

Compassion and sympathy are two very important attributes, although they are distinct. To be sympathetic for someone means to have consideration and understanding without any sort of action. On the other hand, to have compassion is to sympathize and take action concerning the problem or dilemma. I strongly believe both are important and essential. Notice in the above scripture that Jesus was moved with compassion and healed their sick. He wasn't selective and did not question the history of everyone who was present, He simply moved with compassion.

So what kind of sickness and disease are you or your loved ones battling? Perhaps it's cancer, leukemia, rheumatoid arteritis, kidney disease, hypotension, high cholesterol, mental illness, diabetes, blood disease, sickle cell disease, lung disease, or heart disease, or maybe you're struggling with some other circumstance. Psalm 34:19 says, "Many are the afflictions of the righteous, but the Lord delivers him out of them all." The Lord is compassionate and sympathetic. He's never intimidated by any sickness or circumstance. We must remember that human inability is God's opportunity.

📖 Further reading, meditation, and study—Matthew 14:13–21; 1 Peter 3:8–12

DON'T RECEIVE THE MAIL

Casting down arguments and every high thing that exalts itself
against the knowledge of God, bringing
every thought into captivity
to the obedience of Christ.
—2 Corinthians 10:5

While being employed by the United States Postal Service as a letter carrier from time to time, I picked up mail from customers that was marked "return to sender." It was basically return mail that customers felt served no purpose or just wanted to send back. This was their way of communicating to their letter carrier that they did not want to receive it, or that they refused to accept it. Similarly, there are times when we receive bad reports, negative information, or doctor's diagnoses that are not God's will for our lives. When we're confronted with those moments, we must reject the mail.

The Bible says that "death and life are in the power of the tongue, and those who love it will eat its fruit" (Proverbs 18:21). Some years ago, doctors who were on different career paths told me I had cancer. There were two major problems with their medical opinion; I had no surgery and no specimen lab work completed. Their prognosis came from years of combined medical experience without medical data. Both were extremely confident in what they thought would be my outcome. To bring balance here, I appreciate physicians' knowledge and expertise, but for me it was a matter of whose report I was going to believe.

During my medical visits back and forth to the doctor's office, I could never allow my mouth to come into agreement with them.

Hebrews 10:23 says, "Let us hold fast the confession of our hope without wavering, for He who promised is faithful." As it was, all of my tests came back negative. I didn't have cancer, but it could have gone the other way had I come into agreement with their prediction. I owe all praise and glory to the Lord. The thing we should bear in mind is that when we're faced with life's difficulties and are going through manifold trials, we must confess the Word over our circumstances and reject all negative mail.

✧✧✧

 Further reading, meditation, and study—Proverbs 18:21; Philippians 4:6–9

ACCEPTED IN THE BELOVED

Having predestined us to adoption as sons by
Jesus Christ to Himself, according
to the good pleasure of His will, to the
praise of the glory of His grace by
which He made us accepted in the beloved.
—Ephesians 1:5–6

Many years ago, a young man explained to me how he coped with being joked about and laughed at in high school. He was the target of everyone's jokes and laughter. To counteract his experience, he would joke in return to divert the attention away from him. As we continued to talk, his countenance changed, and his eyes began to tear up. I could feel his pain and discerned that he had a spirit of rejection. Interestingly enough, I later ran into someone I knew from high school that reminded me of him. When I greeted him, he treated me with a cold shoulder. You see, I was one of those immature teenagers in high school who didn't know the impact that laughing at jokes would later have on someone's life.

It appears the former classmate had developed a spirit of rejection as well, but unlike the young man who was dejected, his response was one of animosity. But getting back to the young man, I explained how the Lord loves him and has accepted him. I went on to say that he didn't need the approval of people for acceptance and validation. In addition, I explained how the Lord doesn't accept or discriminate against us on the basis of race, appearance, social status, or education. Our acceptance rests solely on the basis of what Jesus did at the cross. It is a finished work, and we're now "accepted in the beloved [Christ]" (Ephesians 1:6).

After I ministered to him and our conversation ended, with tears of joy I could see a noticeable change. He was liberated from the spirit of rejection. What is the opposite of rejection? Acceptance! At the cross, there was a wonderful exchange; Christ was rejected that everyone who feels unworthy and rejected might have acceptance with the Father through Him. Isaiah 53:3 says, "He [Christ] is despised and rejected by men, a man of sorrows and acquainted with grief, and we hid as it were, our faces from Him; He was despised, and we did not esteem Him." When God said we're accepted in the beloved, He's not tolerating or just putting up with us; He has accepted us in Jesus.

✧ ✧ ✧

Earthly friends may prove untrue, doubts
and fears assail; One still loves and
cares for you. One who will not fail. Jesus
never fails, Jesus never fails
Heav'n earth may pass away, but Jesus never fails ...[5]

 Further reading, meditation, and study—Isaiah 53:3–5; Ephesians 1:3–6

CONTINUAL PRAISE

I will bless the Lord at all times His praise shall
continually be in my mouth… I sought the Lord, and He heard
me, and delivered me from all my fears.
—Psalm 34:1, 4

David wrote Psalm 34 during an extremely low point in his life. King Saul wanted to destroy him, and as a result, this sent David on the run, hiding in caves and remote places. Saul was obsessed with destroying David; He literally hunted him down like a bird. (See Lamentations 3:52.) On one occasion, out of desperation, David attempted to join himself to King Achish of Gath. Unfortunately, one of the king's servants disclosed information regarding David's reputation, referring to 1 Samuel 21:11, which says, "Saul has slain his thousands, and David his ten thousand."

This incident resulted in David taking drastic measures, in which he pretended to be a madman in order to join the king's camp. But even under these circumstances and everything he was experiencing, David was able to write, "I will bless the Lord at all times His praise shall continually be in my mouth" (Psalm 34:1). So what caused David to praise God under such immense pressure and circumstances? The fact that David would bless the Lord at all times suggests it wasn't circumstantial praise or even emotional praise, but reverential praise.

Paul and Silas had a powerful time of ministry, and by the power of the Holy Spirit, Paul cast a demon out of a slave girl that was possessed with the spirit of divination. This landed them in jail, but that didn't prohibit their worship and praise to God. (See Acts 16:22–25.) In contrast, many Christians who find themselves in trying circumstances cease their praise and complain instead. Similarly to David, Paul, and Silas, we must know that our help comes from the Lord. This will ensure that we're always praising God in spite of the storms of life that come our way.

✧ ✧ ✧

 Further reading, meditation, and study—Psalm 34:1–3; Psalm 100:1–5

COME TO HIM

But the Lord waits for you to come to Him so He can show you
His love and compassion. For the Lord is
a faithful God. Blessed are those
who wait for Him to help them.
—Isaiah 30:18 (NLT)

The Israelites had disappointed the Lord once again. This time they chose to seek human counsel instead of divine counsel. They had developed a secret alliance with Egypt to throw off the yoke and oppression of Assyria. What's more, they put their dependence upon the Egyptians' chariots, as if horses would ensure their victory, rather the strong arm of the Lord. But they soon realized they needed the Lord's help, and He was patiently waiting. (See Isaiah 30:16–18.)

Likewise, there are multitudes of well-meaning believers in Christ who do not necessarily operate in the same way as the Israelites but who have a distorted view of God the Father. Instead of knowing Him as a loving, holy, righteous, and compassionate Father, they see Him as a tyrant who enforces human-made religious rules—a Father that's quick to judge and punish, and one who's not concerned about their spiritual or physical well-being.

Unfortunately, this false narrative has also led them to believe they cannot come to Him in times of testing, trouble, and need. So, as an alternative, they place their trust and confidence in humanity or seek other means of assistance. Psalm 118:8 says, "It's better to trust in the Lord, than to put confidence in man." After failed attempts of trusting humankind, many realize it's best to come to the Lord. Hebrews 4:16 says, "Let us come boldly to the throne of grace, that we may obtain mercy and find grace to help in time of need." He's waiting with open arms as a father waits for a child; He will never disappoint us.

✧ ✧ ✧

 Further reading, meditation, and study—Isaiah 30:1–8; Matthew 11:25–30

EPIDEMIC OF LONELINESS

Turn Yourself to me, and have mercy on me, for I am
desolate [lonely] and afflicted.
—Psalm 25:16

The Hebrew word translated as "desolate" in the Old Testament means "lonely, one alone, one who is solitary, forsaken, wretched." I cannot think of anyone during Biblical times who has felt the sting of loneliness more than David. While experiencing despair, he makes an earnest appeal to God. Consider what provoked David to write Psalm 25. He was betrayed by his own son in an attempt to overthrow the throne. As a result, the men of Israel went after Absalom, and David was forced to flee his home. For a season he became a lonely and afflicted man.

Some experts have indicated that at least 33 percent of people suffer from chronic loneliness worldwide. I'm not completely sure whether that percentage is accurate, but if it's correct, we have an epidemic of loneliness. It's important to note that there's a vast difference between being alone and being lonely. An individual can be alone without being lonely, and someone can be lonely in a crowded room. To put it another way, you can live in a metropolitan city surrounded by multitudes of people and still experience loneliness.

Therefore, we can conclude that loneliness is a state of mind, an emotion brought on by feelings of separation from other human beings. That said, there are multitudes of people who are experiencing loneliness. So what was David's ultimate response to loneliness and affliction? He chose to cry out and plead the Lord's mercy and intervention. Jesus is the answer to loneliness; He is a friend that sticks closer than a brother. As if that's not enough, He promises us that He will never leave us or forsake us.

✧ ✧ ✧

 Further reading, meditation, and study—Psalm 25:16–22; 2 Timothy 4:9–16

IN HOPE BELIEVED

For in You, O Lord I hope, You will hear,
O Lord my God ... And now
Lord what do I wait for? My hope is in You.
—Psalm 38:15; 39:7

I believe that as we approach the end times, we'll begin to witness scores of hopeless people, especially the unsaved. There are three possible explanations for why there are many miserable and hopeless people in our society. First, hope does not arise from our desires or wishful thinking, but from God, who is the believer's hope. Second, hope is not in an unforeseeable future of things that's not the will of God. And finally, it's important to keep in mind that hope is directed toward the future and is anchored in the realm of the mind. Additionally, it's an attitude of expectancy concerning things that are yet to be.

"The story is told of a great, never-say-die general who was taken captive and thrown into a deep, wide pit along with a number of his soldiers. In that pit was huge pile of horse manure. 'Follow me,' the general cried to his men as he dove into the pile, 'There has to be a horse in here somewhere!'"[6] This fictional story is quite humorous but shows how hope anchored in the mind will help us believe in the impossible even when there's no hope in sight.

In the Old Testament, David endured manifold circumstances that would have caused many to collapse under the weight of them. But what kept him was his hope in the Lord. "And now, Lord what do I wait for? My hope is in You" (Psalm 39:7). Although we may feel like we're being inconvenienced by having to wait, there's a

59

catchphrase I often hear: "He may not come when we want Him to, but He's always on time." Similar to the general who had hope when there was none in sight, we, too, must have that same mindset that things will work out for us.

✧✧✧

 Further reading, meditation, and study—Psalm 38:15–22; Romans 4:13–22

ATTITUDE OF TRUST

In God is my salvation and my glory; the rock of my strength, and
my refuge is in God. Trust in Him [God] at
all times, you people; pour out your
heart before Him God is a refuge for us.
—Psalm 62:7–8

The word "trust" appears at least 132 times in the Bible and is often
mistaken or confused with the word "faith." The difference between
the two is that faith is an act, while trust is an attitude. In other
words, after we have received a word or stepped out in faith, "trust"
describes our attitude moving forward. There's one important thing
we should strive to do as it relates to trusting God, and that is that we
must trust the Lord with all our hearts and at all times. (See Psalm
62:8; Proverbs 3:5.) However, the following story describes how we
don't always fully trust God in the process: "In the Philippines the
driver of a carabao wagon was on his way to the market when he
overtook an old man carrying a heavy load. Taking compassion on
him, the driver invited the old man to ride in the wagon. Gratefully
the old man accepted. After few minutes, the driver turned to see
how the man was doing. To his surprise he found him still straining
under the heavy weight, for he had not taken the burden off his
shoulders."[7]

We can learn much from the story above. Consider Abraham,
who initially struggled trusting God to bring the promise to fruition.
Abraham and Sarah struggled to wait, so instead they decided to do
things their way. They birthed Ishmael instead of Isaac. The good
news as time progressed was that he learned how to trust God. Later

on, the Bible said he was "Fully convinced that what He [God] had promised He [God] was also able to perform" (Romans 4:21). To be fully convinced is to have an attitude of trusting God in spite of what we see, hear, or feel. Instead of an occasional circumstantial trust, we must have an attitude of trust in the Lord.

✧✧✧

 Further reading, meditation, and study—Psalm 62:1–8; Proverbs 3:1–6

WEARY SOLDIERS

Consider Him [Christ] who endured such opposition from sinful men so that you will not grow weary and lose heart.
—Hebrews 12:3 (NIV)

In the natural realm, in order for soldiers to fight in combat, they need strength and perseverance or else they will grow weary and lose heart. Similarly, there are multitudes of Christians who, because of cares of life, marital problems, tribulation, financial difficulties, and circumstances, have become weary soldiers. The devil is fully aware of this, so he intentionally seeks out the weak, frustrated, disillusioned, and spiritually exhausted. As a defensive measure and stance against the devil, the Bible cautions us to "Be sober, be vigilant; because your adversary the devil walks about like a roaring lion, seeking whom he may devour ..." (1 Peter 5:8).

Are you familiar with the National Geographic channel? There's much we can learn watching this program as it relates to the strategies of the devil. Take, for instance, a lion that crouches down and hides in the grass from his prey. Along comes a herd of antelope moving at a fast pace, and in the far distance comes a weak, frail antelope. The dust clears, and there appears the lion. The weak prey is no match for the aggressive big cat. Likewise, Christians who become weak and vulnerable are no match against the assaults of the devil.

Although Paul faced many trials and obstacles over the span of his ministry, he never allowed discouragement and frustration to overtake him or cause him to leave God. Although he had many setbacks, was constantly persecuted, and had companions who intentionally walked away, he remained steadfast and dependent on

63

the Lord. Had he not remained sober and vigilant, the devil and his adversaries would have taken advantage of him. Those who have become weak and weary must never try to fight the enemy in their own strength. They must allow Jesus to strengthened them and fight their battles.

✧ ✧ ✧

 Further reading, meditation, and study—Matthew 11:25–30; Hebrews 12:1–3

SPIRITUAL STAMINA

Have you not known? Have you not heard?
The everlasting God, the Lord.
The Creator of the ends of the earth, neither
faints nor is weary, His understanding is
unsearchable. He gives power to the weak,
and to those who have no
might He [God] increases strength.
—Isaiah 40:28–29 (NIV)

A television documentary I recently watched pointed out that the cheetah survives on the African plains by running down its prey. Although the cheetah is extremely big, it can sprint seventy miles per hour, but the cheetah cannot sustain that pace for long. Within its long, sleek body is a disproportionately small heart, which causes the animal to tire quickly. Unless the cheetah catches its prey in the first flurry, it must abandon the chase.

Similarly, many Christians seem to have the cheetah's approach to ministry and life circumstances. They speed into assignments and projects with great zeal and energy. As it relates to overcoming trials, tribulations, and circumstances, many even start out believing God can bring about the impossible. But as time goes on, they eventually succumb to lack in the heart for sustained effort or faith to believe, determined that if they would run harder and believe more, that would solve their problems.

But what they need may not be more speed or faith but more stamina and endurance, which come only by depending and waiting on the Lord. Isaiah 40:31 says, "Those who wait on the wait on the

Lord shall renew their strength, they shall mount up with wings like eagles, they shall run and not be weary; they shall walk and not faint." We're encouraged further in Scripture to "run with endurance the race that is set before us" (Hebrews 12:1). My friend, it's important that you and I understand it's not how we start out in this spiritual race, but how we finish, that matters the most.

✧ ✧ ✧

 Further reading, meditation, and study—Isaiah 40:28–31; Hebrews 12:1–3

UNCONDITIONAL LOVE

May you experience the love of Christ, though it is so great you will never fully understand it. Then you will be filled with the fullness of life and power that comes from God.
—Ephesians 3:19 (NLT)

The Bible is unquestionably and undeniably the most remarkable and extraordinary book in the universe. It is the greatest love story ever written to humankind. Our salvation would not be possible had not God bestowed upon us His unconditional love by sending His only begotten Son to die in our place. God's love is beyond comprehension and past understanding. (See Ephesians 3:17–19.) Love is not only one of God's attributes; it's also an essential part of His nature. Deuteronomy 7:7–8 says, "The Lord did not set His love on you nor choose you because you were more in number than any other people, for you were the least of all peoples; but because the Lord loves you …"

This scripture context has parallels and reiterates God's unconditional love toward humankind. His love is not based on our social standing, family lineage, or anything of that nature, but His pure, unconditional love for us. Not understanding God's unconditional love will birth a spirit of abandonment and rejection. Have you ever heard the term "dysfunctional home?" There are multitudes of Christians who are dysfunctional because they have not fully comprehended the love of God. So what do they do? They stay in a perpetual state of discouragement and frustration, always struggling to find acceptance and love from others.

As Christians in our developmental years, there was one thing we knew from the very beginning—the Lord Jesus loves us. This was communicated while we attended children's Sunday school class:

> Jesus loves me this I know / for the Bible tells me so /
> Little ones to Him belong / they are weak but He is
> strong /
> yes, Jesus loves me,
> yes, Jesus loves me,
> yes, Jesus loves.

The facts are still the same; we must still know and embrace that simple truth, for nothing "shall be able to separate us from the love of God which is in Christ Jesus our Lord" (Romans 8:39). Have you ever heard the old phrase "You can't beat God giving"? I would add to that by saying "You also can't beat God loving."

📖 Further reading, meditation, and study—Ephesians 3:14–19; 1 John 4:7–16

Weapons of Praise

Now when they began to sing and to praise, the Lord set ambushes against the people of Ammon, Moab and Mount Seir, who had come against Judah; and they were defeated.
—2 Chronicles 20:22

The Bible makes it very clear that we'll face all kinds of adversities and trials in this life. Paul warns us that "we must through many tribulations enter the kingdom of God" (Acts 14:22). What's even more, Jesus said, "In this world you will have tribulation, but be of good cheer, I have overcome the world" (John 16:33). The verb form of "cheer" means "applaud"—another way to say "praise." In other words, no matter what we experience or endure in this life, we must have continuous praise in our mouths.

In the Old Testament, king Jehoshaphat came under attack from a multitude of people. From reading this account, we can learn a few helpful tips on how to remain positive in the midst of circumstances. Instead of Jehoshaphat feeling sorry for himself or throwing in the towel, he turned to God. Second Chronicles 20:18, 22 says, "And Jehoshaphat bowed his head with his face to the ground, and all Judah and the inhabitants of Jerusalem bowed before the Lord, worshipping the Lord … Now when they began to sing and to praise, the Lord set ambushes against the people of Ammon, Moab, and Mount Seir, who had come against Judah; and they were defeated"

Now keep in mind that Jehoshaphat did not appoint snipers, gunmen and swordsmen. He didn't have a military strategy or plan, nor did he call for reinforcements. He simply put together a spiritual

69

praise team. The moment they began to praise and their praises reached heaven, the Lord immediately moved on their behalf. We all have prayer at our disposal, but we must never forget we have the weapon of praise in our spiritual arsenal as well. Praise invokes the intervention of God, because man's inability is God's opportunity.

✧ ✧ ✧

 Further reading, meditation, and study—2 Chronicles 20:1–30; Psalm 34:1–10

GOD'S FAITHFULNESS

Therefore, know that the Lord your God,
He is God, the faithful God
who keeps covenant and mercy for a thousand
generations with those who love
Him and keep His commandments.
—Deuteronomy 7:9

The word "faithfulness" means "dependability, loyalty, and steadfastness." This perfectly describes some of God's attributes. He is dependable, loyal, and steadfast. Lamentations 3:22–23 says, "Through the Lord's mercies we are not consumed, because His compassions fail not. They are new every morning, great is Your [God's] faithfulness." It's important to note and understand that God's faithfulness is not contingent upon our personal desires and wants, just as His responses do not come based on when we think He should answer us.

We must bear in mind that God's timing is important, but can we wait and trust Him in the process? Do we believe He will answer our prayers? Remember the old catchphrase "He may not come when you want Him but He's always on time." Some years ago, I was going through a very trying time with a health issue, I needed God's intervention and healing. The Lord promised that He would bring me through in spite of the doctor's prognosis. I am happy to say that when the dust cleared, so to speak, in His faithfulness, God had healed and delivered me.

Trust should be our response to God's faithfulness. The Bible says, "Trust in the Lord with all your heart, and lean not on your

71

own understanding …" (Proverbs 3:5). My friend, we can trust Him with all our heart because we know He will never let us down, He will never disappoint us, and He will never forsake us. What's even more, in 2 Timothy 2:13 we're told, "If we are faithless, He remains faithful; He cannot deny Himself." You really have to digest the notion that God remains true to Himself. Even when we disappoint Him, He remains faithful.

✧ ✧ ✧

 Further reading, meditation, and study—Deuteronomy 7:6–9; Lamentations 3:22–26

GRACIOUS WORDS

You [Jesus] are fairer than the sons of men;
grace is poured upon Your lips
therefore God has blessed You forever ... So all
bore witness to Him [Jesus], and marveled at
the gracious words which proceeded out of His mouth ...
—Psalm 45:2; Luke 4:22

One of the characteristics I love and admire about Jesus during His time on Earth is His ability to communicate effectively. He was a master at using the right words and knowing how to communicate with people. While on Earth, His life was one of truth, holiness, love, compassion, transparency, honesty, candidness, and bluntness. When He spoke, the people around Him were amazed; even His enemies had to take notice. Matthew 7:28–29 says, "And so it was, when Jesus had ended these sayings, that the people were astonished at His teaching, for He taught them as one having authority, and not as the scribes."

Jesus knew the importance of speaking with love and humility, but He also knew how to speak with boldness and authority. What set Him apart from His peers was a lifestyle that backed what He said and taught. When it came to living a life of holiness and truthfulness, His counterparts the Pharisees and the religious leaders were a total contradiction in light of how Christ lived. Jesus took the opportunity to be bold at various times when He spoke and responded to the people, but He was also very gracious with His words.

It's not enough just to speak the truth; it has to be done in a gracious manner. The psalmist gives a good description of how Jesus communicated: "You are fairer than the sons of men; grace is poured upon Your lips; therefore, God has blessed You forever" (Psalm 45:2). The NIV translation of the latter part of that verse reads, "Your lips have been anointed with grace." When Jesus bids us to come to Him, that should never be a struggle, because we'll never be met with rejection and contempt, but with mercy and grace that have poured from His lips.

✧ ✧ ✧

 Further reading, meditation, and study—Psalm 45:2–7; Luke 4:16–22

MORE THAN ENOUGH

For you are becoming progressively acquainted
with and recognizing more strongly
and clearly the grace of our Lord Jesus Christ (His kindness,
His gracious generosity His undeserved favor and spiritual
blessing in that though He was so very rich, yet
for your sakes He became so very poor in order
that by His poverty you might become
might become enriched abundantly supplied.
—2 Corinthians 9:8 (AMP)

Many years ago, believers in the body of Christ were reluctant about embracing the prosperity messages and blessings of God. From what I know, there are two things that may have contributed to that mentality: religious tradition and doctrinal teaching. As a result, many Saints rejected the concept of God prospering and blessing them. Thanks be to God that since that time there has been a vast improvement with the way Saints believe and think in the church. A transformation of the mind has truly taken place.

The thing we must bear in mind is that there's is an unlimited, never-ending, superabundant overflow of grace, mercy, and provision in God. The well of God never dries up. His resources never diminish. You and I have an open grace account with God through Christ Jesus—full and overflowing for every need and more. "So," you ask, "how can I access or withdraw from this account?" All you need is faith; it is the withdrawal slip. And grace is the account number, fugitively speaking.

Philippians 4:19 says, "But my God shall supply all your need [spiritually, emotionally, physically] according to His riches in glory by Christ Jesus." Whatever we ask or think according to God's will, He's able to do exceedingly more. (See Ephesians 3:20.) God wants to bless us far more than we can think or even imagine—far beyond our religious mindsets and far beyond our expectations and limitations. There's no limit to what God can do. The problem never lies with Him, but in our ability to believe and trust Him. We must always remember God is omnipotent; He's absolutely powerful!

✦✦✦

 Further reading, meditation, and study—2 Corinthians 9:6–8; Ephesians 3:20

BREAKTHROUGH PRAYERS

So I say to you, ask and it will be given to
you; seek, and you will find; knock
and it will be opened to you. For everyone who
asks receives, and he who seeks finds
and to him who knocks it will be opened.
—Luke 11:9–10

Prayer is one of the greatest opportunities, one of the greatest privileges, and one of the greatest ministries available to all Christians. Have you noticed there's nothing recorded in the Bible that suggests Jesus taught the disciples to preach or teach? But one important thing He taught them was how to pray. That alone shows us the importance of prayer. The Bible points out different types of prayers. Prayers may consist of praise, thanksgiving, worship, intercession, supplication, petition, warfare, and breakthrough.

Breakthrough prayers are not so much about asking for things, which is the main focus of petition prayers, but rather about addressing a situation or circumstance. They involve a refusal to give up until the answer comes. It's similar to the man who had a pressing need at midnight and kept knocking until his friend opened the door. (See Luke 11:5–8.) Praying for a breakthrough often comes with a cost—a cost that requires a process of toil, travail, and labor. James 5:16 says, "The effective fervent prayer of a righteous man avails much."

When we need a breakthrough, we must knock until our answer comes. Just ask the widow in Luke 18; she wasn't going home until the unjust judge granted her request. At the beginning of that chapter, Jesus said something that is the clarion call for those who want a breakthrough; He said, "men always ought to pray and not lose heart" (Luke 18:1). What was He saying? We should never give up and continue to pray until we get an answer. Have you ever noticed that Jesus commended those who were persistent? If you are in need of a breakthrough, faith and persistence are the keys.

✧ ✧ ✧

  Further reading, meditation, and study—Luke 11:5–13; James 5:13–18

ABBA FATHER

For you did not receive the spirit of bondage
again to fear, but you received
the Spirit of adoption by whom we cry out,
'Abba Father.' The Spirit bears witness
with our spirit that we are children of God.
—Romans 8:15–16

The word *"Abba"* is an Aramaic word that corresponds to "Daddy" or "Papa." God is our Abba Father, He's our Father, Daddy, or Papa. We are extremely blessed with the privilege of calling God our Father. "Behold what manner of love the Father has bestowed on us, that we should be called children of God ..." (1 John 3:1). To this day, in some parts of the Middle East, the children call their natural father "Abba father." They know that their father will meet all their needs. But there are multitudes of people who are looking for a father. Some are fatherless because their natural father is no longer living or not presently active in their lives.

Consequently, many go into search mode, trying to fill that void by joining gangs, clubs, secret societies, fraternal groups, civic organizations, country clubs, and so on. Others look for a spiritual father, pastor, or mentor. Although some relationships have their place, no one is more important than our Heavenly Father. We have the privilege of calling Him our Father, and the fact that He sees us as sons and daughters is absolutely astonishing. The benefit of belonging to the best family in the universe, is that we lack nothing (Psalm 23:1; Philippians 4:19). We have extraordinary benefits, but there's one in particular we can appreciate.

Our Heavenly Father's love for us is unconditional, and without His example and demonstration of it, we would not be able to give or have a revelation of love. (See Romans 5:5–6.) Unfortunately, there are natural children who grow up without knowing love because they did not experience it through their earthly parents. But we can look to our Heavenly Father. He is the author and definition of love. (See 1 John 4:7–8.) The Bible says we have been given everything according to life and godliness, and none of it would be possible had God not bestowed His unconditional love upon us. His love is beyond comprehension and past our understanding.

✧✧✧

 Further reading, meditation, and study—Romans 8:12–17; 1 John 3:1–3

HE RESCUES

The Lord hears His people when they call
to Him for help. He rescues
them from all their troubles. The Lord is close
to the brokenhearted; He rescues
those who are crushed in spirit.
—Psalm 34:17–19 (NLT)

The effects of a wounded spirit can traumatize a person for many years. Even some in the church have become wounded, especially from authoritarian and legalistic abuse. Someone who has a wounded spirit will feel helpless and frustrated. Consider Rebekah, Isaac's wife, who, because of frustration, said, "I am weary of my life … what good will my life be to me" (Genesis 27:46). These are the kinds of statements they speak, not realizing that "Death and life are in the power of the tongue, and those who love it will eat its fruit" (Proverbs 18:21).

Our spirits, souls, and bodies can be adversely affected. Through a series of unfortunate events or circumstances, the spirit can become wounded. Proverbs 18:14 says, "The spirit of a man will sustain his infirmity; but a wounded spirit who can bear." We humans can overcome some physical injuries, and we can even overcome and sustain (bear, tolerate, endure, withstand, and weather) an illness or disease. But when the spirit is wounded, every area in our lives can be affected. Here are a few proactive things a person can do to move forward after being wounded in his or her spirit.

One of the ways to overcome a wounded spirit is by praying to the Father. "The Lord hears His people when they call to Him for help … He rescues those who are crushed in spirit" (Psalm 34:17–19). Another way an individual can overcome a wounded spirit is by reading and meditating on the Word of God. Psalm 107:19–20 says, "Then they cried out to the Lord … He sent His word and healed them." And finally, we must cast all of our problems, burdens, and pain upon the Lord. Psalm 147:3 says, "He [Christ] heals the brokenhearted and binds up their wounds." Jesus is the answer for all of humankind's problems and needs!

✧ ✧ ✧

 Further reading, meditation, and study—Psalm 34:4–19; 2 Timothy 4:9–18

ADVERSITY TO PURPOSE

We are assured and know that [God being
a partner in their labor] all things
work together and are [fitting into a plan] for good
to and for those who love God and are
called according to [His] design and purpose.
—Romans 8:28 (AMP)

Military boot camp prepares ordinary people to become combat-ready soldiers. I can recall when a group of us arrived at a military base in Fort Dix, New Jersey. None of us looked like soldiers, and I'm quite sure none of us felt like military soldiers. In subsequent weeks to come, we would have to endure many tough obstacles and all sorts of training through our drill sergeant. It didn't make any difference where we came from or what we were prior to boot camp; when it was all said and done, we were transformed into United States military soldiers.

I remember our drill sergeant singing a cadence that went like "Momma, momma, can't you see / what the army done to me / momma, momma, can't you see / what the army done to me." What we were singing as we kept in step was based on pure facts, because there was a noticeable change in all of us when we left the military camp and relocated to our permanent-duty stations. We weren't the same civilians (or, as in my case, immature teenagers) that arrived at the training station on buses. The adversity and training had transformed us into military soldiers.

The Bible says that when David was chosen by God to succeed King Saul, "the Spirit of the Lord came upon David from that day forward" (1 Samuel 16:13). Although he became Saul's successor by Samuel anointing him, the promotion wasn't going to happen overnight. In fact, he went back to tending his father's sheep. Why? because he had to endure a season of preparation and hardships to step into his purpose. The same holds true for us; we must be prepared for whatever God has purposed in our lives. It's then that we can yield a peaceable fruit.

📖 Further reading, meditation, and study—1 Samuel 16 chapter; 2 Samuel 2 chapter

GARMENT OF PRAISE

To comfort all who mourn, and provide for those
who grieve in Zion to bestow on them
a crown of beauty instead of ashes, the oil of gladness
instead of mourning, and a garment of
praise instead of a spirit of despair. They will
be called oaks of righteousness, a
planting of the Lord for the display of His splendor.
—Isaiah 61:3

In the above scripture reference, there are some key elements that describe what some Christians are enduring or feeling at this moment. Phrases like "to comfort all who mourn," "provide for those who grieve," "oil of gladness instead of mourning," and "a garment of praise instead of a spirit of despair" (or, as some translations say, "a spirit of heaviness"). Praise is one-size-fits-all, and it should be worn as a garment. It fits us and looks good on us. We should wear it often, because it counteracts a heart of mourning and despair.

The Bible encourages us to put on certain things. For instance, we must put on spiritual armor, the armor of light, Christ, the new man, the garment of praise, and so on. This gives us the understanding that the burden of responsibility falls on us. Not only is giving God praise the right thing to do, but it looks good on us, it's presentable, and it's beautiful. Psalm 147:1–2 says, "Praise the Lord! For it is good to sing praises to our God; for it is pleasant [loving, pleasing] and praise is beautiful. The Lord builds up Jerusalem; He gathers together the outcasts of Israel, He heals the brokenhearted, and binds up their wounds."

Most Christians' understanding of praise is somewhat vague. To some it means offering up mechanical, robotic, unemotional lip service to God. But praise is more than formalism and mere lip service, because it also releases healing. When we praise the Lord, it takes our attention off ourselves and our circumstances. According to Psalm 147:2 and Isaiah 63:3, there are remedies for the spirit of despair, a broken heart, and a wounded person. When we choose to put on the garment of praise, we'll find there's healing and deliverance.

✧✧✧

 Further reading, meditation, and study—Psalm 147:1–7; Isaiah 61:1–3

WEATHERING THE STORM

The righteous cry out, and the Lord hears,
and delivers them out of all their
troubles ... Many are the afflictions of the righteous. But the Lord
delivers him out of them all.
—Psalm 34:17, 19

There are similarities between a natural storm and a spiritual storm. For instance, when a natural storm comes, dark clouds gather and move in over a city. It suddenly becomes dark, the winds blow, the trees swing, it rains, it thunders, and there are intermittent flashes of lightning. But after a storm comes in, it eventually comes to an end and moves on. Shortly thereafter, everything becomes quiet, the clouds clear up, the sun comes out, the birds sing, and a sweet aroma fills the air.

Did you visualize or see what I shared? Because that's similar to what takes place after we have endured a spiritual storm. Please pay close attention to the portion of the scripture above that says, "Many are the afflictions of the righteous" (v. 19). This gives us reason to believe that in this life we will face many various types of afflictions or storms. But as we read on, it says, "But the Lord delivers him out of them all" (v. 19). So it appears we may have to weather the storm for an extended period, but the good news is that "weeping may endure for a night, but joy comes in the morning" (Psalm 30:5).

Consider the woman who had a spirit of infirmity for eighteen years, the man with an infirmity for thirty-eight years, and the widow who needed justice from her adversary. They had at least one thing in common—they weathered the storm and got their breakthroughs. And finally, remember Peter; as long as he kept his eyes on Jesus, he was able to walk on water in spite of the raging storms around him. And how about Paul, who was on a loaded ship in the midst of a raging storm, but God delivered him and the men as well? Just remember that God will do the same for us if we cast all our cares on Him.

✧✧✧

Not every storm that comes into your life is intended to disrupt your life, some come to clear your paths.

 Further reading, meditation, and study—Psalm 30:1–5; Psalm 34:4–22

DELAYED BUT NOT DENIED

Then the Lord answered me and said; write
the vision and make it plain on
tablets that he may run who reads it. For the vision
is yet for an appointed time; but at the
end it will speak, and it will not lie, though
it tarries, wait for it; because it
will surely come, it will not tarry.
—Habakkuk 2:2–3

Every believer in Christ has to endure seasons of waiting. The end purpose is to build our faith and character. It's during these times that pride is exposed, and trust in our resources and ability is stripped away. We're learning how to depend solely on God. While we're enduring our season of waiting, there's a peace that comes with knowing that nothing the devil tries to do can abort the plan of God. When the Lord speaks a word or gives us a promise, it's like a seed that needs time to sprout. The timing of God is essential in our season of waiting, and similar to how a seed grows, God knows when we have reached the time of germination, the time of fruition.

When patiently waiting for the promise to come into fruition, we must take into account that God is a God of order. What I mean is that He has a predetermined appointment to release certain things in our lives. Instead of seeing the process of waiting as an inconvenience, we should embrace it as a blessing. When we're placed on hold, those are the times when things seem silent. We ask God when things will happen, but God's response is not always yes or no; sometimes He says, "Not now!" Or He may say, "Wait!" That is not the answer many of us want to hear. We want God to say, "Go, make haste, attack the purpose," and so on. But He just might say, "Not now!" Or He may say "Wait!"

For instance, when a commercial airline plane is unable to land, the airline traffic controller will instruct the pilot to wait in the air. To wait in the air means to assume a holding pattern until further instructions come from the tower. During this time, the plane is flying in circles around the tower. That's how many of us may feel at times—like we're going nowhere, just going in circles. But our waiting is not in vain. When we hear the Lord say, "Assume a holding pattern until further notice," He is doing something very special behind the scenes. Remember: God's ways are beyond our comprehension, and all things do work together for our good. The promise being delayed doesn't mean the promise is denied.

📖 Further reading, meditation, and study—Habakkuk 2:2–3; Hebrews 6:13–20

REMEMBER HIS BENEFITS

Bless the Lord, O my soul; and all that is
within me, bless His holy name!
Bless the Lord, O my soul, and forget not all His
benefits. Who forgives all your iniquities
Who heal all your diseases. Who redeems your
life from destruction? Who crowns
you with lovingkindness and tender mercies ...
—Psalm 103:1–5

After retiring from the military, I was told to make an appointment to visit my nearest veterans' hospital for a routine medical exam. At the time, I was a very young man, in my early twenties. While walking with my wife through the hospital corridor, an older gentleman approached me and pulled my wife and me to the side and said, "Young man, are you a military veteran?" I responded with "Yes sir." With that, he went on to say, "You need to know your veterans' benefits, because no one is going to tell you about them." After we finished talking, he walked away and turned back toward us, stating emphatically, "Make sure you read about your benefits."

I will never forget that brief encounter with that older gentleman. Through subsequent years, that brief conversation in the hallway of a VA facility would help me in many ways. Because of his counsel, I later discovered I had some valuable benefits because of my military service. According to Psalm 103:2, David wrote, "Forget not all His [God's] benefits." I must point out that God's benefits are more valuable than any natural benefits. Similar to the advice I was told to read about my natural benefits, I'm encouraging you to read the

Bible and discover there are valuable benefits you may be forfeiting that are available because of Christ.

But unfortunately, for whatever reason, many Christians are claiming only a portion and have rejected certain benefits in the Bible. This is perhaps due to religious tradition, legalism, a personal belief, or even a denominational doctrinal belief. Whatever the reason is, David admonishes us to not forget all of God's benefits. Notice that David emphasizes the word "all." Not only should we not forget them all, but when we fully embrace them all, they're guaranteed.

✧✧✧

Standing on the promises of Christ my King,
Through eternal ages let His praises ring!
Glory in the Highest I will shout and sing
Standing on the promises of God![8]

 Further reading, meditation, and study—Psalm 103:1–5; Ephesians 1:3–11; 2 Peter 1:2–4

A Clean Slate

For as the heavens are high above the earth, so great is His mercy
toward those who fear Him; as far as the
east is from the west, so far
has He removed our transgressions from us.
—Psalm 103:11–12

No one should ever feel condemned and guilty but rather convicted after hearing the gospel of Christ. There's a vast difference between condemnation and conviction; the Holy Spirit has an important role in separating the two. His job is to bring about conviction, not condemnation. John 16:8 says, "And when He [Holy Spirit] has come, He will convict the world of sin, and of righteousness, and of judgment." Furthermore, after the Holy Spirit convicts us and we repent, we should not continue on with feelings of shame and guilt.

Should an individual feel guilty after carrying out acts of sin? Certainly! A guilty conscience should prompt a person to repent. (See 1 John 1:9.) However, when we confess and repent of our sins and still struggle with guilt and condemnation, that suggests we are not fully liberated. Remember: Jesus said, "If Son makes us free, we shall be free indeed" (John 8:36). We must not allow the devil to invite us to a pity party of dwelling on our past mistakes. 1 John 3:21 says, "Beloved if our heart does not condemn us we have confidence toward God."

The key phrase here is "We have confidence toward God." The devil knows that if he can keep us in a perpetual state of guilt and condemnation, our confidence toward God will be greatly affected. All of us have skeletons in the closet, so to speak, and that's where they should stay buried. But a heart full of condemnation and guilt will keep opening the closet and letting out the skeletons. We must know, the moment we confess and repent of our faults and sins to God, it's done. "As far as the east is from the west, so far has He removed our transgressions from us." God doesn't keep a record of sins that have been forgiven. He has wiped the slate clean.

✧ ✧ ✧

 Further reading, meditation, and study—Psalm 103:8–12; 1 John 1:5–9

DEBILITATING STRONGMAN

For God has not given us a spirit of fear, but of power and
of love and of a sound mind.
—2 Timothy 1:7

God hasn't given us the spirit of fear, so who imparts this debilitating strongman? Satan, of course! Paul cautioned Timothy to not be afraid, because God had given him power, love, and a sound mind. The spirit of fear will neutralize or kill the initiatives and purposes of God in our lives if allowed. Fear has a way of causing people to sabotage their own God-given assignment on their lives. The word "sabotage" means "to damage, disrupt, interrupt, impair and incapacitate." Not only will the spirit of fear neutralize and kill the purpose of God, but it can also cripple people in a variety of ways.

For instance, I read a story about a woman who was afraid of coming out at night even to attend church. The pastor finally convinced her to come to a night service. Upon her going to the altar for prayer, the spirit of fear was cast out of her through the power of the Holy Spirit. After the service, they looked for the woman that had been delivered and found out that she had walked home alone, unafraid, in the dark, singing as she went. When she arrived at her front door, she turned around and walked some more in the dark night.

The spirit of fear no longer had influence over her life. Fear was replaced with confidence, boldness, and courage. Similarly to that woman, the Lord wants us to experience victory in every area of our lives, "for God did not give us a spirit of timidity (of cowardice, of craven and cringing and fawning fear), but [He has given us a spirit] of power and of love and of calm and well-balanced mind and discipline and self-control" (2 Timothy 1:7 AMP). Please pray the prayer below, asking God to destroy the spirit of fear in your life or the lives of your loved ones.

✦✦✦

Father, in the name of Jesus I take my stand
against the spirit of fear that's
trying to operate in my life. Bind and destroy any
demonic powers that are trying to take
over my mind, my thinking, and my heart.
Dismantle them in the name of Jesus
Christ. I refuse to operate in fear. I uproot
it in the name of Jesus. Let the fire
of the Holy Spirit fall upon the enemy's camp
in the name of Jesus. I loose myself
and my family and cast out the spirit of fear
right now in Jesus's name. Amen!

 Further reading, meditation, and study—Psalm 46:1–3; Luke 12:4–7; 2 Timothy 3–7

Fruit of Joy

But the fruit of the [Holy] Spirit [the work
which His presence within
accomplishes] is love, joy (gladness), peace,
patience (an even temper, forbearance)
kindness goodness (benevolence), faithfulness,
gentleness (meekness, humility)
self-control (self-restraint, continence), against such there is no law
[that can bring a charge].
—Galatians 5:22 (AMP)

It's no secret there are multitudes of people in society who don't experience, or lack, joy. Unfortunately, many believers struggle to demonstrate joy in their lives as well. Because joy is one of the fruits of the Spirit, it can be smothered and lie dormant. Let me explain further. Many Christians are praying for joy but already have it; they just don't demonstrate in their lives. Every single fruit listed in the book of Galatians is crucial for the believer. Personally, I believe love is the primary fruit that bonds and facilitates all the other fruit of the Spirit. But joy is the catalyst and driving force behind our actions, interactions, and behavior.

Please notice the positions of love and joy in the above scripture reference; they're numbers one and two in the list, respectively. The fruit of joy is essential in our witness behavior while we are enduring circumstances, interacting with people, and exhibiting our passion and desire while carrying out kingdom service. Basically, joy is a positive attitude or pleasant emotion; it's vastly distinct from worldly happiness. The joy that Christians have is holy and uncontaminated.

There are many levels of joy that are mentioned in the Bible, including gladness, contentment, and cheerfulness.

But there's one very important thing we should know about joy, and that is that true Biblical joy is not the absence of trials or tribulations, but choosing, rather, to rejoice in the Lord in spite of our circumstances. There's an old phrase that goes "Don't let no one steal your joy," but I love the one even more that goes, "This joy that I have—the world didn't give it, and the world can't take it away." Oh, how true that is; the Holy Spirit is the one who imparts the fruit of joy. There's a song entitled "Love is an Action Word" by Witness that say, "Love isn't love until it's given away." My friend, I would add that joy isn't joy until we demonstrate it in our lives.

✧✧✧

 Further reading, meditation, and study—Nehemiah 8:9–10; Galatians 5:22

WORKING TOGETHER

We are assured and know that [God being
a partner in their labor] all things
work together and are [fitting into plan] for good
to and for those who love God and are
called according to [His] design and purpose.
—Romans 8:28 (AMP)

When I consider things that come together for good, the ingredients and end result of a cake come to mind. Every single ingredient is important in making a scrumptious cake, but those ingredients are not good if consumed separately. However, if you mix everything together and place the ingredients in a cake pan, followed by a hot oven, everything works together to bring about a delicious and scrumptious cake. That is similarly what circumstances and trials accomplish in our lives. When things seem to be working against us, they are actually working together for our good.

The story of Joseph in the Old Testament is a great example of how bad things can work together for the good. At the outset, everything seemed contrary to his dreams; instead of going forward toward his destiny, Joseph was spiraling backward. Instead of a quick promotion as a result of his dreams, he was on a path of suffering. (See Psalm 105:17–19.) However, when the dust finally cleared, all things worked together for Joseph's good. Genesis 45:5 says, "But now, do not therefore be grieved or angry with yourselves because you sold me here; for God sent me before you to preserve life."

We can be comforted knowing the painful ingredients of life, so to speak, are just setups. They are stepping stones for what God wants

99

to accomplish in and through us. Behind the curtains of heaven, God is constructing something beautiful in us. (See Philippians 1:6.) Prior to a butterfly becoming a beautiful insect, it must go through a metamorphic stage to transform into something lovely. That's what's happening to us when all things are working together. At first it doesn't seem as if something is happening, but we're changing slowly into completely different people by way of a spiritual metamorphic process.

✧ ✧ ✧

 Further reading, meditation, and study—Genesis 45:1–28; Romans 8:28

JOY OF SALVATION

Create in me a clean heart, O God, and renew a steadfast spirit within me. Do not cast me away from Your presence, and do not take Your Holy Spirit from me. Restore to me the joy of Your salvation and uphold me by Your Generous Spirit.
—Psalm 51:10–12

Throughout the Bible, there are individuals who fall from grace; King David is one of those people. He committed terrible acts of sin by committing adultery with Bathsheba and arranging the murder of her husband, Uriah. After being confronted with his transgressions by the prophet Nathan, he had godly sorrow and immediately came to a realization that he needed God's mercy, forgiveness, and restoration. In his brokenness, he said "Restore to me the joy of Your salvation, and uphold me by Your Generous Spirit" (Psalm 51:12).

Fortunately for David, God restored him and forgave him of all his transgressions. Jesus promised us that he would forgive us and release us from the stain and guilt of sin when we confess and repent. First John 1:9 says, "If we confess our sins, He is faithful and just to forgive us our sins, and to cleanse us from all unrighteousness." The only exception He mentions is blasphemy against the Holy Spirit. (See Matthew 12:31–32.) If we sin without repenting, we forfeit the joy of salvation. Committing acts of willful sin deprives us of living victorious lives in Christ.

God is in the business of restoring His servants. He takes no pleasure in His children losing the joy of His salvation. If Peter were here today, he would share his testimony of how Jesus restored him, even after denying knowing Him following the resurrection. The horrible sin of denying and knowing Jesus must have weighed him down, similar to David saying that his sin was always before him. (See Psalm 51:3.) We must always remember we can come to Jesus when we sin, because He wants complete fellowship with us.

✧✧✧

Father God, I believe You sent Jesus to die for my sins. I believe Jesus has risen from the grave and is now seated at Your right hand, making intercession for us; and on that basis, I believe Satan's claim against me is cancelled. Similar to the prodigal, I have sinned against You and hurt those who love me. I have fallen from grace; please forgive me for my rebellion and restore me back to the place from which I have fallen. I thank You for Your long-suffering, grace, and mercy toward me. I humbly ask all of these things in Your Son Jesus's name. Amen!

 Further reading, meditation, and study—Psalm 51:1–10

AMAZING GRACE

Amazing Grace! How sweet the sound,
that saved a wretch like me!
I once was lost, but now am found
was blind but now I see.
T'was, Grace that taught my heart to fear,
and grace my fear relieved;
how precious did that grace appear;
the hour I first believed![9]

"In the summer of 1994, Marcio da Silva, a lovestruck Brazilian artist, was distraught over the breakup of a four-year relationship with his girlfriend, Katia de Nascimento. He tried to win back her love by a gesture of great devotion. He walked on his knees for nine miles. With pieces of car tires tied to his kneecaps, the twenty-one-year-old man shuffled along for fourteen hours before he reached her home in Santos, Brazil. He was cheered on by motorists and passersby, but when he reached the end of his marathon of love thoroughly exhausted, the nineteen-year-old woman of his dreams was not impressed. She had intentionally left her home to avoid seeing him."[10]

The story of the lovestruck Brazilian artist is a reminder to everyone that trying to impress God and earn salvation through works is useless. Salvation is the bestowment of God's grace and the atonement of Christ, not sacrificial works. In Paul's letter to the believers at Ephesus, he explains that God's grace is the source of our salvation. Ephesians 2:8 says, "For by grace are ye saved through faith." Notice that he never said faith was the source or that we're saved on the account of our faith. Faith is the channel through which salvation flows, and grace is the fountain or stream that flows through that channel.

Faith is the aqueduct down which the flood of mercy flows to refresh our thirsty souls. An aqueduct is a water system that was developed in Rome to carry water into the city. It was important that it stayed intact in order to carry the constant flow of water. Likewise, our faith must be genuine that it may become a solid channel of mercy to our souls. We should bear in mind that faith is only the channel or aqueduct and not the fountainhead. The salvation of the Lord can come to us even though our faith is that of a mustard seed, because the power lies in the grace of God and not in our faith.

📖 Further reading, meditation, and study—John 1:14–17; Ephesians 2:1–10

EMERGENCY SYSTEM

In my distress I called upon the Lord, and cried unto my God
He heard my voice out of His temple, and my cry came
before Him even into His ears.
—Psalm 18:6 (KJV)

The 911 emergency system is a state-of-the-art system. All that is required is to dial the numbers, and you'll be immediately connected to a dispatcher. Similarly, when we dial (in prayer) the throne of grace, we are immediately connected to God. Psalm 3:4 (KJV) says, "I cried unto the Lord with my voice and He heard me out His holy hill, Selah." In front of every dispatcher, there is a readout list of telephone numbers, addresses, and the names by which each call is connected with that address.

Likewise, God knows us by name, and as Paul told the Athens men, God "Has determined their pre-appointed times and the boundaries of their dwellings" (Acts 17:26). Jesus said He knows those who are His sheep and is ready to answer their petition in prayer. Psalm 34:15, 17 says, "The eyes of the Lord are upon the righteous, and His ears are open unto their cry … The righteous cry, and the Lord heareth, and delivereth them out of all their troubles." When someone communicates with a dispatcher, there are others who are listening as well: police, firefighters, and paramedics.

Likewise, the Father, the Son, and Holy Spirit are listening and ready to assist us in our troubles. There is time lost when an individual calls into a dispatcher but is unable to explain his or her problem. It could be someone who is having a heart attack and cannot speak calmly with the dispatcher. Similarly, there will be times in our lives when we're in desperate situations that require 911 prayers to be dialed to the throne of grace. It's comforting to know that Jesus is our Great High Priest. We can always approach the throne of grace. Psalm 46:1 (KJV) says, "God is our refuge and strength, a very present help in trouble."

✧ ✧ ✧

 Further reading, meditation, and study—Psalm 18:1–6; Psalm 34:4–7

MIDNIGHT NEED

And I say unto you, ask and it shall be given you; seek
and ye shall find; knock and it shall be opened unto you.
For everyone that asketh receiveth; and he that seeketh
findeth and to him that knocketh it shall be opened.
—Luke 11:9–10 (KJV)

In the Gospel of Luke, Jesus shares a story about a man who shows up at a friend's house during midnight hours. His request is for three loaves of bread, because a friend of his had traveled far to visit. But because the friend and his children are in bed, the man's request is denied. However, because of the man's determination and persistence, his request is finally granted. (See Luke 11:5–10.) This story is figurative of God's grace and mercy in response to the prayers of those in need. The Bible says we should "come boldly to the throne of grace, that we may obtain mercy and find grace to help in time of need" (Hebrews 4:16).

It's important to point out that the loaves of bread were not for the man who came at midnight but for a friend of his. There will be times during prayer when we go to the throne of grace boldly not for our own personal needs but to intercede for the needs of others. We set aside our requests for those who need urgent help. Philippians 2:4 says, "Let each of you look out not only for his own interests, but also for the interests of others." The man's dilemma wasn't an ordinary need but a need that required prompt attention and assistance. This is clearly seen because he comes at an inopportune time, for his friend and his friend's family were in bed.

This story gives us assurance and comfort in knowing that,

contrary to the friend's reluctance to help, God never sleeps or slumbers. (See Psalm 121:4.) Notice again how the friend in need was very persistent and never gave up. Likewise, we're encouraged to be persistent and expectant when we pray to the Father. Jesus said, "Men always ought to pray and not lose heart" (Luke 18:1). The reason we should never give up is because the Lord is always available and willing to supply our needs. (See Psalm 23:1; Hebrews 10:23, 35.) My friend, when we operate in faith and with an unrelenting determination, it gets the attention of heaven.

✧ ✧ ✧

Whenever we learn the importance of
praying for the interests of others—
the body of Christ and the world—instead of
our immediate personal needs, our
intercession and supplication, God will honor our prayers.

 Further reading, meditation, and study—Luke 11:5–13; Hebrews 14–16

SECOND CHANCES

For a righteous man may fall seven times and rise again …
If we confess our sins, He is faithful and
just to forgive us our sins and
to cleanse us from all unrighteousness
—Proverbs 24:16; 1 John 1:9

Peter was very outspoken and wrought many miracles by the power of God. But early in his walk with God, he made some costly mistakes. For instance, his first mistake was attempting to walk on water but looking at the problem instead of Jesus. (See Matthew 14:29–31.) This happens quite often to the best of us. We start out excited and enthusiastic but quickly take our eyes off Jesus when we encounter problems. Peter's second mistake was having a preconceived notion about what the Lord was sent to do. He tried to convince Jesus to cancel the plan of God. (See Matthew 16:21–23.) Many Christians struggle with the sin of presumption as well. Believing they have everything figured out, they take matters into their own hands.

Peter's third mistake came when he took matters into his own hands by striking a high priest's servant to save Jesus. (See John 18:7–11.) Many Christians struggle with this as well; they lean on their understanding and don't always acknowledge the Lord. (See Proverbs 3:5–6.) Finally, Peter's fourth mistake was his denial of any association or tie to Jesus. (See John 18:15–18.) Although Paul was very adamant about how he was not ashamed of the gospel, there are many modern-day Christians who are, especially around family, friends, and coworkers. Peter's mistakes brought him to an extreme low point in his life. He had just denied his master, the one he witnessed being falsely accused and sentenced to death.

But the Lord is in the business of forgiveness and restoration. Peter didn't have to go looking for Jesus; He came looking for him. This is grace and mercy restoring people at its best. Peter did not deserve restoration, but mercy and grace appeared. In spite of all his mistakes and failures, God still raised him up to be an apostle to the Jews; and on the day of Pentecost, he preached to three thousand souls. He stood up again not in denial of Christ but in the power of God. It's absolutely a blessing to know Jesus still leaves the ninety-nine and goes after those who have fallen from grace. God is a restorer of people and a God of second chances!

✧✧✧

    Further reading, meditation, and study—Proverbs 24:15–16; John 21:15–19

UNHEALTHY CODEPENDENCY

For when one says, I am of Paul, and another, I am
of Apollos, are you not carnal? Who then is Paul,
and who is Apollos, but ministers through whom
you believed, as the Lord gave to each one?
—1 Corinthians 3:4–5

There are a number of churches and organizations that foster an unhealthy codependency toward spiritual leadership. Many believers struggle in their personal relationship with the Lord or reading and studying their Bibles. So, with not being spiritually rooted and grounded in the Word of God and their relationship with God, they turn their attention toward leadership. This, of course, simplifies the process for some leaders who are dogmatic, controlling, and legalistic in nature. Unfortunately, the end purpose that they are trying to achieve is to control every aspect of their members' lives.

Looking back at the cults that have risen over past and recent years, we see a pattern they have in common. Each group is an island to itself that has a primary leader who is accountable to no one but himself or herself. The followers simply worship the ground he or she walks on. Paul addresses this futile need to worship a man by asking this important question: "Who then is Paul, and who is Apollos, but ministers through whom you believed, as the Lord gave to each one?" (1 Corinthians 3:5). Jim Jones is a prime example of what goes wrong when people place men in positions they should not be in. His followers worshipped and depended on him, and as a result, they would do practically anything he told them to do.

There's good news: God has placed safety barriers in the Bible

111

to prevent unhealthy codependences from occurring. I understand and appreciate what Paul meant when he wrote, "looking unto Jesus the author and finisher of our faith" (Hebrews 12:2). Thank God for our spiritual leaders and spiritual mentors, but we must never place them before the Lord. They're just holy men and women who are used by God. We must have spiritual discernment, sight, and hearing. Remember that Jesus said, "My sheep hear My voice, and I know them, and they follow me" (John 10:27). If we completely surrender to the Holy Spirit, He will guide and lead us.

✧✧✧

 Further reading, meditation, and study—Jeremiah 17:5–8; John 10:27; 1 Cor. 3:4–7

No Hidden Clauses

Bless the Lord, O my soul, and forget not all His benefits
who forgives all your iniquities, who heals
all your diseases, who redeems
your life from destruction …
—Psalm 103:1–4

Between the pages of the Bible, there are exceedingly great promises that are established on a better covenant. (See Hebrews 8:6.) We must claim them and receive them. Similarly to an insurance policy, we must take time to read and receive what's been freely given to us. The difference between an insurance policy and the Bible is that in most insurance policies there's fine print. In my understanding, the small writing is intentional; it's meant to discourage you from further reading about your rights and benefits.

In contrast, the Word of God is distinct, for there's no fine print; everything is right in front of us to see, read, and claim. There are No hidden clauses, rights, or benefits. Second Corinthians 1:20 (NIV) says, "For no matter how many promises God has made, they are 'Yes' in Christ." Additionally, what's so wonderful is the fact we have Jesus as our Mediator; He will make sure every promise and benefit is ours to have. First Timothy 2:5 says, "For there is one God and one Mediator between God and men, the Man Christ Jesus."

So what are you struggling with or experiencing? Remember to go back and read the Biblical policy (the Bible). As a matter of fact, David said we must "not forget all of His [the Lord's] benefits" (Psalm 103:2). And here's one other important thing we should know, unlike an insurance policy, which changes, renews, expires, or fluctuates, the Lord and His promises remain the same. Psalm 119:89 says, "Forever O Lord, Your Word us settled in heaven. Your faithfulness endures to all generations."

✧ ✧ ✧

 Further reading, meditation, and study—Psalm 103:1–5; Hebrews 8:1–6

UNDERGIRDING GRACE

Abide in Me, and I in you. As the branch
cannot bear fruit of itself, unless it
abides in the vine, neither can you, unless
you abide in Me. I am the Vine
you are the branches. He who abides in
Me, and I in him bears much
fruit; for without Me you can do nothing.
—John 15:4–5

Every believer in Christ has been anointed to carry out an assigned task or purpose from God. In other words, when God saved us, we were called for a specific purpose and "created in Christ Jesus for good works, which God prepared beforehand that we should walk in them" (Ephesians 2:10). What's more, we have been given everything we need that pertains to life and godliness to carry out this great work. Second Corinthians 9:8 (KJV) says, "And God is able to make all grace abound toward you; that ye always having all sufficiency in all things, may abound to every good work."

Because we are created to do good works, we must be totally dependent upon God's undergirding grace. Allow me to explain what that means. The word "undergird" denotes support or strengthening. First, everything we undertake for God requires guidance and direction from the Holy Spirit. Secondly, we need God to undergird (support or strengthen) us with His grace. There are multitudes of believers in the body of Christ who are burned out from doing things—or should I say carrying out religious activity—without God's undergirding grace.

They seek to serve God in this way, but over a period of time it becomes a struggle for them to maintain. One of the ways we know we're operating in the flesh instead of being led and empowered by the Spirit is that we're always frustrated and exhausted. Frustration and exhaustion are red flags and are indicators that God's grace and the Spirit's empowerment are not on what we're doing. They could be good things but are not authorized by God. We must always be totally dependent on Jesus, because without Him we can do nothing.

Basically, God tends to put us in position for which we are not qualified. The reason being, He doesn't want us to rely on our own ability. It is not according to our works; but it is according to His grace ... Grace begins where human ability ends. If you can do it by yourself why should God give you His grace?[11]

📖 Further reading, meditation, and study—John 15:1–5; 2 Corinthians 9:8

ASK OF HIM

Now this is the confidence that we have in Him, that if
we ask anything according to His will He hears us. And
we know that He hears us, whatever we ask we know
that we have the petitions that we have asked of Him.
—1 John 5:14–15

I cannot think of someone who does not want God to bless him or
her in some way, but there are those who are afraid or hesitant to
ask Him. But mentioned in the Old Testament is an honorable man
named Jabez, who wasn't reluctant in asking God to bless him. First
Chronicles 4:9 says, "Jabez was more honorable than his brothers,
and his mother called his name Jabez, saying because I bore him in
pain." The literal meaning of his name means "he will cause pain."
Consider the meaning of his name; it had negative consequences and
a bleak future attached to it.

I believe Jabez knew that if God would bless him, it would
counteract every single negative consequence that awaited him.
According to verse 10, "Jabez called on the God of Israel saying, oh,
that You would bless me indeed, and enlarge my territory, that Your
hand would be with me, and that You would keep me from evil, that
I may not cause pain. So God granted him what he requested." First,
Jabez called on God. This is always the first step toward receiving
from the Lord. We must ask; we will not receive if we do not ask.
(See James 4:3.)

There are some Christians who might see Jabez's request as
spiritually immature. They may even say, "After all, it appears he's
only concerned about himself." Statements like that are why many

are reluctant to ask God to bless them. They believe these types of requests come off as arrogant, vain, and egotistical. We must always bear in mind that we can ask God to bless us, without the dread of feeling guilty or inconveniencing Him. (Luke 11:9–10.) According to what we know from the Bible, a desire to prosper in every area of our lives is a good thing. (See 3 John 1:2.) God stands ready to answer our prayer requests.

📖 Further reading, meditation, and study—1 Chronicles 4:9–10; 1 John 5:14–15

GRACE IS NOT WEAK

That in the ages to come He might show the exceedingly riches of His grace in His kindness toward us in Christ Jesus. For by grace you have been saved through faith...
—Ephesians 2:7–8

Grace is not weak or fragile. In fact, it's quite the opposite. It's magnificent, powerful, and, as John Newton's song says, amazing. Christians who operate and are bound by legalism cringe when they hear the word "grace." I believe the reason why they respond in that way is because it exposes at least two things: self-righteousness and pride. It exposes self-righteousness because they seek to establish their own righteousness and pride because God resists the proud but gives grace to the humble. (See Romans 10:3; 1 Peter 5:5.)

Allow me to highlight a few reasons why grace is so important. First, grace helps us in times of weakness and need. (See Hebrews 4:14–16.) Second, grace plays an important role in carrying out service in the kingdom of God. (See Hebrews 12:28.) Third, grace has a major role in calling men and women to ministry. (See Galatians 1:13–16.) Fourth, grace extends mercy when communicating to and with others. (See Colossians 4:5–6.) Last, but certainly not least, the grace of God brings salvation. (See Ephesians 2:4–9; Titus 2:11.)

So as you see, grace is not weak or fragile; it dismisses any argument or rationale from those who don't comprehend the role and beauty of it. If it had not been for God's mercy and grace, where would any of us be? Because of the grace of God and Jesus, who is full of grace and truth, we can certainly appreciate what Paul meant when he confessed, "But by the grace of God I am what I am, and

His grace toward me was not in vain ..." (See 1 Corinthians 15:10.) The next time anyone tries to minimize the effectiveness of grace, tell him or her that by the grace of God we are who we are.

✧ ✧ ✧

 Further reading, meditation, and study—1 Corinthians 15:9–10; Ephesians 2:1–10

RESET

For a righteous man may fall seven
times and rise again ...
—Proverbs 24:16

There are multitudes of believers in Christ who have failed in some area and feel they disappointed God. The cares of life and costly mistakes have discouraged and disheartened them. The apostle Peter knew what it meant to greatly disappoint the Lord. Right before the crucifixion and resurrection of our Lord Jesus, he denied ever having any association with or knowing Him. (See John 18:15–18.) Peter was at a very low point in his life, but after the resurrection, Jesus restores him back to his place in Him. (See John 21:15–19.) Since Peter was granted a second chance, he was able to reset, or start over again.

Katherine Kuhlman, the late healing evangelist, overcame setbacks and failures. Through the help of the Holy Spirit, she was able to reset and start over again. Early in her ministry, it seems, everything was going well—until she made a bad decision that caused her to lose everything. A couple of years later, she decided to start over again. That meant she would have to come to the end of herself and walk away from someone she loved dearly. After the dust cleared and she pushed the reset button, things drastically changed for the better. She became a national and world-renowned healing evangelist whom God used powerfully in her later days.

The word "reset" means "to adjust again after initial failure," "to set anew," or "to set again." What that says to us is that as long as we're able to breathe in air, it's never too late to start again. My friend, if you have fallen from grace, confess and repent and pick yourself up from where you have fallen. First John 1:9 says, "If we confess our sins, He [Christ] is faithful and just to forgive is our sins and to cleanse us from all unrighteousness." No matter what kind of bad choices we have made in this life that have caused us to fail, because of the grace and mercy of God, we can always reset and start again.

✦ ✦ ✦

God can restore what is broken and change it into
something amazing. All you need is faith!

 Further reading, meditation, and study—Proverbs 24:15–16; John 21:15–19

PROVISION FOR PURPOSE

And God is able to make all grace abound toward you,
that you always having all sufficiency in all things,
may have an abundance for every good work.
—2 Corinthians 9:8

A preacher once said that purpose is our responsibility but provision is God's responsibility. Whatever God's objectives and purposes are, He provides for them. To say this another way, whatever God commissions us to do, we can be assured the purpose has built-in provision. For instance, a story was told by the late televangelist R. W. Schambach, who set up tents for his meetings at a time in his ministry when he really needed to upgraded his trucks to haul his equipment around the country. The big trucks he presently had were old and struggling.

During a meeting one night, the Lord instructed him to give one of his trucks away to a preacher on the platform. The next day, he received a phone call from his secretary informing him that there was a man who was retiring in his office. According to the man, she told Schambach that God instructed him to give his eighteen-wheeler tractor-trailer truck to him because he had been called to full-time ministry. This story shows us how God will provide for the purposes and missions He calls us to.

Exodus 3:21 says, "And I will give this people favor in the sight of the Egyptians and it shall be, when you go that you shall not go empty-handed." Why did God allow the Israelites to acquire so much material wealth from the Egyptians? If you look closely, you'll see that later on God instructed them to build a tabernacle in the wilderness so that He could dwell in it. Exodus 25:8 says, "And let them make me a sanctuary that I may dwell in." The testimony of Schambach and the story of the Israelites, among others, show us that whatever we're called to do, the purpose has a built-in provision; we don't have to worry, because God will provide.

✦✦✦

 Further reading, meditation, and study—2 Corinthians 9:8; Philippians 4:19

DESPERATE MEASURES

*And when they could not come near Him [Christ]
because of the crowd they uncovered the roof where
He was. So when they had broken through they let
down the bed on which the paralytic was lying.*
—Mark 2:4

Have you ever got to the point of desperation and cried out to the Lord in faith because of a medical condition? Throughout the Gospels, there are people who do just that. Their cries released tremendous faith that was often recognized and commended by Christ. Maybe you never experienced something of that magnitude, but there are some circumstances that require desperate and radical appeal. An incident that highlights this is the story of a paralytic. (See Mark 2:1–9.) I can envision the paralytic saying to the four men that assisted him, "Can you please carry me to Christ? I heard He heals the sick."

In fact, he wasn't ready to lie down in defeat, waiting for a healing meeting to come into his town. He had made up his mind that whatever it would take to receive healing, he was willing to do it. Interestingly enough, in this life there are people who need healing but choose to wait for a particular preacher or healing meeting to come to their area. They sort of remind me of the man in the Gospel According to John who had a spirit of infirmity. Instead of approaching the throne of grace boldly and asking for help in his time of need, he waited thirty-eight years for others to help him. (See John 5:1–15.)

The good news is that we don't have to wait for someone to help

125

us or healing meetings with long lines to come to our cities or towns. All we need is faith that Christ will heal and deliver us. Matthew 21:22 says, "And whatever things you ask in prayer, believing, you will receive." Faith never waits to see before it believes, because facts don't change the Word of God. The Word of God changes the facts. We can always approach the throne of grace with boldness and confidence that we may find grace to help in time of need.

✧ ✧ ✧

 Further reading, meditation, and study—Matthew 9:27–31; Mark 2:1–9

FINISHED WORK

I have glorified You on the earth, I have finished the work
which You have given Me to do. And now, O Father glorify
Me together with Yourself, with the glory which I had with
You before the world was ... He [Christ] said, it is finished
—John 17:4–5, 19:30

When we speak about the benefits and blessings of Calvary, we cannot omit the word "redemption." In light of the finished work, we are redeemed from every curse—body, soul, and spirit, solely through the atonement of Christ. The word "redemption" speaks of salvation, deliverance, liberation, and recovery. Jesus recovered through His death on the cross what Adam, through his rebellion, had caused us to lose. Adam, by his fall, opened the door for sin, disease, and sickness. But Jesus took our infirmities and bore our sicknesses and was manifested to "destroy the works of the devil." (See Matthew 8:17; 1 John 3:8.)

The greatest barrier in the minds of those seeking bodily healing in this dispensation is the uncertainty of whether or not healing is God's will. Matthew 8:17 says, "That it might be fulfilled which was spoken by Isaiah the prophet, saying: He Himself took our infirmities and bore our sicknesses." In addition, 1 Peter 2:24 says, "Who Himself bore our sins in His own body on the tree, that we, having died to sins might live for righteousness—by whose stripes you were healed." These scriptures and more establish the fact that divine healing is the Father's will for His children.

It's baffling to the mind to think that many people seldom question anything in a natural contract or policy but refuse and reject many things in the Bible—especially divine healing and so on. The atonement of Christ has paved the way for many important benefits. (See Psalm 103:2–3.) But it's up to us to embrace them. In 1 Peter 2:24—the latter part, where it says "were healed"—this speaks of the fact that Jesus's experience on the cross was a finished work. And as a result of that finished work, we have exceedingly great and precious promises. One of those precious promises or important benefits is divine healing.

✧✧✧

 Further reading, meditation, and study—Matthew 8:1–17; Mark 5:21–43

Rolled Away

Then the Lord said to Joshua, this day I have rolled
away the reproach of Egypt from you. Therefore, the
name of the place is called Gilgal to this day.
—Joshua 5:9

Under Moses's leadership and the Lord's guidance, the Israelites were freed from generations of slavery and oppression from the hands of Egyptians. On their way to their ancient homeland, these refugees— or should I say generational farmers—had no understanding about warfare. At some point during their long, arduous journey, some men were chosen and trained to assist Moses. Among those leaders and the most gifted of them was Joshua. He was very important in assisting Moses on important missions and assignments.

Joshua led the defense of troops in the famous battle, while Moses stood on the hillside with his staff raised. A man named Hur and Moses's brother Aaron held up his hands until sunset. The successes Joshua achieved in battle earned him his new name from Hoshea. It was only Joshua who went to Mt. Sinai with Moses, where he spent forty days and nights in God's presence. Joshua was chosen to represent his tribe, Ephraim, on the spy team to survey the land. When Moses disobeyed God, Joshua was officially recognized as Israel's leader.

Having shared a few historical facts concerning Joshua's victories and achievements, according to the Lord, he still had one problem that needed to be resolved: "The Lord said to Joshua, this day I have rolled away the reproach of Egypt from you" (Joshua 5:9). The word "reproach" means "shame and disgrace." The reproach Israel had was the idolatry of the Egyptians, which brought about their disgrace and wandering in the wilderness. When God saved and delivered us, He removed the reproach (shame, guilt, and disgrace) of sin off of us. Old things passed away, and all things became new.

✧✧✧

 Further reading, meditation, and study—Joshua 5:8–12; 2 Corinthians 5:17

HEART MATTERS

But the Lord said to Samuel, do not look at his appearance
or at his physical stature, because I have refused him. For
the Lord does not see as man see; for man looks at the
outward appearance, but the Lord looks at the heart.
—1 Samuel 16:7

Consider the story of David when God chose him to replace a
disobedient King Saul. When Samuel arrived at Jesse's home to pick
a successor for Saul, David was almost overlooked, firstly because he
was out in the sheep pasture, secondly because he was quite young,
and finally because it appeared Samuel had a preconceived notion
about what a king should look like. God had to teach him a quick
lesson of how He chooses a man or woman. 1 Samuel 16:7 says,
"But the Lord said to Samuel, do not look at his appearance or at his
physical stature, because I have refused him. For the Lord does not
sees as man sees; for man looks at the outward appearance, but the
Lord looks at the heart."

Furthermore, this was a time during which Goliath was taunting
the Israelites, and Jesse sent David out to check on his brothers. Upon
arriving, David asked questions about the progress of the war. In
response, his oldest brother said, "Why did you come down here?
And with whom have you left those few sheep in the wilderness?
I know your pride and the insolence [disrespect, rudeness] of your
heart, for you have come down to see the battle" (1 Samuel 17:28).
Please note that God told Samuel he looks at the heart of man. So
clearly God would never have chosen David if his heart were filled
with pride, disrespect, and rudeness, as his oldest brother insinuated.

131

It's not uncommon for someone to be judged or rejected by those close to them. Some of these reasons may include but may be limited to outward appearances, stature, education, social status, family familiarity, and so on. God knows the heart of man. John 2:25 says, "And had no need that anyone should testify of man, for He [Christ] knew what was in man." No matter who rejects, criticizes, disrespects, or judges us, we can take comfort in the fact that our God looks at our hearts and accepts us.

✦ ✦ ✦

 Further reading, meditation, and study—1 Samuel 16:6–13; Matthew 12:33–37

Not My Battle

You will not need to fight in this battle. Position yourselves, stand still and see the salvation of the Lord, who is with you, O Judah and Jerusalem! Do not fear or be dismayed; tomorrow go out against them, for the Lord is with you.
—2 Chronicles 20:17

There are spiritual and natural battles in which we must know and understand the rules of engagement, which may or may not require us to engage. But there are some battles in which we should just stand and trust God for victory. Some years ago, my wife and I were picking up one of my sons, who was on spring break, from Montgomery, Alabama. As usual, we had to wait for our sons to sign out and load the vehicle with their belongings. While we were waiting in the vehicle, in a radio interview I heard a preacher say that people were urging him to jump into a particular battle for something that had happen in a neighborhood near the preacher's home.

They had gotten upset with him because he felt led to forego the fight. He went on to say that his hands were already full and that God would fight for them in this case. The interviewer said "are you okay with how they feel toward you?" His response was, "It doesn't matter what they think, it's what God is saying; there are some battles you don't have to fight." I was listening carefully because I could relate and what he was saying was biblical. The devil will draw you into a fight that's not yours. God told Jehoshaphat to get in place and watch Him fight the battle.

I believe many Christians try to fix things on their own or fight the enemy themselves. Every so often, God has to remind us that "the battle is not yours, but God's" (2 Chronicles 20:15). When we allow that to sink in, we have assurance and peace of mind that everything will be okay. So the next time you encounter life's circumstances or the enemy attacks, pray for direction and guidance and you might hear God say, "You will not need to fight in this battle."

✧ ✧ ✧

 Further reading, meditation, and study—2 Chronicles 20:1–30; Romans 8:26–38

DOUBLE FOR TROUBLE

And the Lord restored Job's losses when he prayed for his friends.
Indeed, the Lord gave Job twice as much as he had before ... Now
the Lord blessed the latter days of Job more than his beginning ...
—Job 42:10, 12

Many people would tell you that when going through traumatic
experiences you'll never see or envision the end unless you see it by
faith. If there is someone in the Old Testament who endured much
pain, it is certainly Job. He was from the land of Uz, a place that may
have been located near Edom. Some Hebrews traditions place him
in Hauran, a fertile area east of the Jordan River. And because his
lifespan is listed roughly around 140 years, he may have lived in the
early patriarchal period.

The Bible records that Job "was blameless and upright, and one
who feared God and shunned evil" (Job 1:1). Not only was he a
righteous man, but he was married and had a large family. What's
more, he was very wealthy; the Bible says he "was the greatest of
all the people of the east" (v. 3). The actual saga of Job's life began
in heaven, when God praised him, saying, "There is none like him
on the earth, a blameless and upright man, one who fears God and
shuns evil" (v. 8). In the following passages, Satan dismisses Job's
impeccable record of faith, stating that God has blessed and protected
him. Immediately after their conversation, Satan launches a massive
attack on Job.

According to the Book of Revelation, Satan is the accuser of
the brethren. Because of that, we can expect similar accusations and
attacks. We must not forget the miserable friends of Job who accused

him and misunderstood his suffering, claiming that God rewards evil with suffering and good with prosperity. Because of Job's refusal to accuse God and his faithfulness, God restored him and gave him double for his trouble. Similarly, we can expect God to restore and bless us when we pass through the waters and walk through the fires of life.

✧✧✧

 Further reading, meditation, and study—Genesis 30:25–43; Job 42:1–10

DELIGHT IN THE LORD

Trust in the Lord, and do good; dwell in the land, and
feed on His faithfulness. Delight yourself also in the
Lord, and He shall give you the desires of your heart.
—Psalm 37:3—4

Has someone ever told you that whatever you desire or want from God, He will give it to you? Of course, that's not Biblical. They base their rationale on where it says, "Delight yourself in the Lord, and He shall give you the desires of your heart" (Psalm 37:4). I was asked some time ago what my interpretation of the above scripture is. The individual who asked me this, thinking like many do, was taken by surprise at my response. I had recently read the scripture and knew God doesn't give us anything we want or desire, because He knows doing so would hurt or destroy us.

I responded that through God's Spirit, He imparts His will, His purpose, and His desire. John 16:14 says, "He will glorify Me, for He [Holy Spirit] will take of what is Mine and declare it to you." In other words, when God's will, purpose, and desire are implanted in our hearts, we pray and petition Him accordingly. As a result, our prayers are not self-centered. James says that if we "ask amiss, we may spend it on our pleasures" (James 4:3). When we're surrendered to the Holy Spirit, our prayers are unselfish, spiritual, and not self-seeking and carnal. Many Christians haven't gotten to this level of understanding.

Many years ago, I can recall a man who was praying for something he could not afford. He was under the impression that if he could pray fervently in the Spirit, God would grant his request. He failed

137

to understand that God's will, not wishful thinking, is of upmost importance. Finally, there's at least one scripture that speaks volumes about delighting ourselves and praying according to His will. 1 John 5:14–15 (NLT) says, "And we can be confident that He [God] will listen to us, whatever we ask Him for anything in line with His will. And if we know He is listening when we make our requests, we can be sure that He will give us what we ask for."

✧ ✧ ✧

  Further reading, meditation, and study—Psalm 37:3–6; James 4:6–10

MAN OF VALOR

And the Angel of the Lord appeared to him [Gideon],
and said to him the Lord is with you mighty man of
valor … Then the Lord turned to him and said, go in
this in this might of yours, and you shall save Israel from
the hand of the Midianites. Have I not sent you?
—Judges 6:12, 14

One important valuable benefit we have as a result of our relationship with the Father is that we come to know who we are. The Father gives us our spiritual identities. You might have heard people say they received their identities from their parents. Some believe they're the ones who let us know our purposes and who we are. The problem with what they're saying is that our earthly parents can only raise us to be good citizens and speak positive things into our lives. Similarly to a warrior that has arrows in his or her hands, they can guide us in the right direction. (See Psalm 127:3–5.) However, our Heavenly Father is the one who gives us our real identities and purposes.

From reading the story of Gideon, I came away with the impression that it's impossible to not know our true identity unless the Father reveals it. Judges 6:15 says, "So he said to him, O my Lord how can I save Israel? Indeed, my clan is the weakest in Manasseh and I am the least in my father's house." God revealed and unveiled to Gideon who he really was. In fact, Gideon's assessment of himself was not how the Father viewed him, because the angel told him, "The Lord is with you, you mighty man of valor" (v. 12). Gideon thought he was the least and the weakest, far from his real identity of a mighty man of valor.

Consider the prophet Jeremiah. God knew him before he was in his mother's womb. Jeremiah 1:5 says, "Before I formed you in the womb I knew you; before you were born I sanctified you; I ordained you a prophet to the nations." Just think for a moment; before Jeremiah's parents decided to have a child, the Lord already knew Jeremiah and his purpose in life. We should be encouraged knowing that our Heavenly Father unveils and reveals who we are and our purposes. (See Acts 9:10–16; Galatians 1:5–16; Ephesians 2:10.) We may not always be accepted, and we may not understand what God is doing, but only He can give us a revelation of who we are.

❖ ❖ ❖

 Further reading, meditation, and study—Judges 6:1–27; Jeremiah 1:1–19

ROOM TO GROW

You did not choose Me, but I chose you and appointed you that
you should go and bear fruit, and that your fruit should remain,
that whatever you ask the Father in My Name He may give you.
—John 15:16

There's one thing all Christians must have in common, and that is
the desire to grow in all phases of the Christian faith—a hunger to
make an impact in the kingdom of God. I learned over the years
that at sundry times in our spiritual walk, God will challenge us to
do more and reach further out. It's similar to what Jesus told Peter:
"Launch out into the deep and let down your nets for a catch" (Luke
5:4). Many years ago, I was given a similar challenge by the Lord
from two complete strangers who said to me, "Don't place God in a
box." I have come to understand this as "Don't limit Him." Below
is a story that sheds some light on this topic.

> Charles Simpson, In Pastoral Renewal, writes; I met a
> young man not long ago who dives for exotic fish for
> aquariums. He said one of the most popular aquarium
> fish is the shark. He explained that if you catch a small
> shark and confine it, it will stay a size proportionate
> to the aquarium. Sharks can be six inches long yet
> fully matured. But if you turn them loose in the
> ocean, they grew to their normal length of eight
> feet. That also happens to some Christians. I've seen
> the cutest little six inch Christians who swim around
> in a little puddle. But if you put them into a larger

141

arena—into the whole creation—only then can they become great.[12]

The above story really speaks volumes regarding how we can limit ourselves and God when we choose to stay in something God wants us to come out of or leave from. We'll never be fully effective and reach our full potentials if we're afraid to launch out into the deep. Be careful of people who try to keep you in their small aquarium or pond when God is calling you to grow in a larger arena. Growing is not just limited to us doing things, but we must grow in the grace and knowledge of our Lord and Savior, Jesus Christ.

✧ ✧ ✧

 Further reading, meditation, and study—Luke 5:4–11; 2 Peter 1:3–11; 3:17–18

OUT OF THE DEPTHS

Out of the depths I have cried to You, O Lord; Lord hear my
voice! Let Your ears be attentive to the voice of my supplications …
I wait for the Lord, my soul waits, and in His word I do hope.
My soul waits for the Lord, more than those who watch for the
morning yes, more than those who watch for the morning.
—Psalm 130:1, 5–6

At some point, we have cried out to the Lord from the depths of our
hearts. Most people, to some degree, are reserved when praying, but
when faced with difficulties and circumstances beyond their control,
they utter cries for help similar to those of David and Jeremiah. David
wrote, "Hear my cry, O God; attend to my prayer. From the end of
the earth I will cry to You, when my heart is overwhelmed; lead me
to the rock that is higher than I" (Psalm 61:1–2). Jeremiah's petition
was "I called on Your name, O Lord, from the lowest pit, You heard
my voice; do not hide Your ear from my sighing, from my cry for
help" (Lamentations 3:55–56).

The book of Psalms is very encouraging when we're battling
circumstances, but many of the psalms David wrote were birthed out
of adversity and pain. One such incident that describes his cry for
help is when he returned to Ziklag only to find it had been attacked
and burned with fire. What's more, all the women and children had
been taken, including his two wives. The good news is that after
inquiring of the Lord, he recovered all. So if there was anyone who
knew how to cry out from the depths of his heart, it was King David.

Some years ago, I was very anxious about the outcome of a
biopsy I had taken at a hospital lab. It seemed that an eternity passed

143

as I was waiting for the results. But while anxiously waiting for a call from my doctor, I stayed on my knees, constantly crying out to the Lord. My prayers were similar to David, who wrote, "... When my heart is overwhelmed; lead me to the rock that is higher than I" (Psalm 61:1). My friend, it's very encouraging to know when faced with circumstances that we can cry out to Lord and He will hear and respond. As it turned out, my results were negative, praise God!

✧ ✧ ✧

Fervent boldness in prayer comes forth when we're confident that the thing we have asked for is according to the will of God.

 Further reading, meditation, and study—Psalm 130:1–8; Lamentations 3:55–57

SPIRITUAL ORPHANS

And I will pray the Father, and He will give you another
Helper [Comforter] that He may abide with you forever ...
I will not leave you orphans I will come to you.
—John 14:16, 18

As believers in Christ, our Heavenly Father is ever present with us
by His Spirit. What's even more, His love for us is everlasting and
unconditional. What that means to us is this: His love is not based on
how we can please Him or how many ceremonial laws or fabricated
rules we can keep. Jesus paid a tremendous price in order for us to
be restored back to the Father. (See John 3:16; Romans 5:1.) As a
matter of fact, according to Paul, "God demonstrated His own love
toward us, in that while we were still sinners, Christ died for us"
(Romans 5:8).

By now you may be asking, "If all of the above is true, why do
we have spiritual orphans?" This is largely because some Christians
have deliberately rejected the gift of the Holy Spirit. As a result,
they have become spiritual orphans who operate out of the flesh and
insecurity. This is one of the reasons Jesus sent back the Holy Spirit—
to counteract many insecurities we would have without Him. The
opposite of insecurity is security. By the Holy Spirit being an ever-
present help in time of need, He accommodates this in our lives.

As a result of things beyond their control, many people have
become natural orphans. However, spiritual orphans intentionally
reject the Holy Spirit and His benefits. On the flip side, Christians
who accept the gift of the Holy Spirit don't have to operate as
orphans, and they rely on the arm of flesh, superficial things, or

fabricated rules. They rely solely on God's provision and security, and they enjoy the benefits that accompany His presence. They know that Jesus said He will never leave them or forsake them.

✧ ✧ ✧

 Further reading, meditation, and study—John 14:15–18; Romans 5:1–5

BETTER PROMISES

But our High Priest [Christ] has been given a ministry that
is far superior to the ministry of those who serve under
the old laws, for he is the one who guarantees for us a
better covenant with God, based on better promises.
—Hebrews 8:6 (NLT)

The benefits we have under the new covenant are far superior to
those of the old covenant. Yet many Christians gravitate back to
the old covenant system of rules, regulations, and laws. Let's take
a moment and look at a few promises as a result of the atoning
work of Jesus at the cross. First, we are the righteousness of God in
Christ. (See 2 Corinthians 5:21.) The moment we receive Christ,
something beautiful takes place—an exchange of our sin for Christ's
righteousness. Christ became sin for us, that we might be made the
righteousness of God in Him.

Second, we have been justified and have access to God. (See
Romans 5:1–2.) There's no more enmity between us and God. Third,
we have been reconciled back to the Father. (See 2 Corinthians 5:18.)
Christ redeeming us back to the Father is the primary reason we're
no longer enemies and strangers. Fourth, we're sealed with the Holy
Spirit. (See Ephesians 1:13.) The moment we are filled with the
Holy Spirit, it validates that we truly belong to the Father. Fifth, we
are God's workmanship created to do good works. (See Ephesians
2:10.) We are God's work of art, His masterpiece, with the purpose
of carrying out good works.

Sixth, we have spiritual fullness in Christ. (See John 4:13–14;
John 6:35.) Jesus says we'll never thirst or hunger again. Finally, we

have obtained an eternal inheritance in Christ. (See Ephesians 1:11; Hebrews 9:15; 1 Peter 1:3–4.) Our eternal inheritance is reserved, unfadable, incorruptible and undefiled. This list doesn't fully exhaust everything we presently have, but I am hopeful it will enlighten Christians who revert back to the old covenant. The atoning work of Christ has blessed us far beyond measure.

✧ ✧ ✧

 Further reading, meditation, and study—Ephesians 1:11–14; Heb. 8:1–6; 1 Peter 1:3–4

Blessing in Disguise

We are assured and know that [God being a partner in
their love] all things work together and are [fitting into
a plan] for good to and for those who love God and
are called according to [His] design and purpose.
—Romans 8:28 (AMP)

The spirit of rejection can derive from a variety of negative
experiences, which can be quite painful and traumatizing. For
instance, an individual can feel rejected when someone's actions,
behaviors, or words are offensive. Offensive words can come in
the form of sarcastic and cynical remarks, rhetorical questions,
unwholesome and unpeaceful dialogue, and so on. When someone
rejects you by actions or words, that person reveals how he or she
feels about you. Remember: Jesus said, "For out of the abundance
[overflow] of the heart the mouth speaks" (Matthew 12:34). We
should never, at any time, minimize the effects that rejection can
have on a person.

Rejection is not always injurious and can be a blessing in disguise
depending on how we view and perceive it. For example, Joseph
being sold by his brothers could be seen as their rejection of him, but
it worked out for Joseph's good. (See Romans 8:28.) When it was
all said and done, Joseph had a positive perspective regarding what
happened to him. Joseph told his brothers, "But now do not therefore
be grieved or angry with yourselves because you sold me here; for
God sent me before you to preserve life … And God sent me before
you to preserve a posterity for you in the earth, and to save your lives
by a great deliverance" (Genesis 45:5, 7).

One time I heard a preacher say that right before an advancement of a promotion comes new levels, and a season of rejection often takes place. He went on to say that God is perhaps elevating you and moving you up, but those who have rejected you cannot go with you. Just think; if the preacher is correct—and I concur—if those people who rejected you had not revealed their hearts to you early on, it could have been very costly to you later on. So we must bear in mind that rejection is not always a bad thing. Perhaps God could be using that experience to move you into your destiny.

✧ ✧ ✧

  Further reading, meditation, and study—Genesis 45:1–8; Romans 8:28

Touching God's Heart

Most assuredly, I say to you, he who believes in Me, the works
that I do he will do also will do also; and greater works than
these he will do, because I go to My Father. And whatever you
ask in My name, that I will do, that the Father may be glorified
in the Son. If you ask anything in My name, I will do it.
—John 14:12–14

Are you fully aware that God knows and sees absolutely everything?
He looks deep within the crevices of our hearts and souls even while
we're praying. Instead of prayers that are self-centered and self-
seeking, regarding which James says, "You ask and do not receive …"
(James 4:3), God is well pleased when we pray for things that are close
and dear to His heart. According to Matthew 6:10, Jesus said we are
to pray, "Your kingdom come. Your will be done on earth as it is in
heaven." One of the highest purposes of prayer and intercession is to
bring glory to God.

However, at times our flesh will contend, contest, and be in
conflict with God's will when we are praying. Those reasons, among
other things, are why we greatly need the help of the Holy Spirit.
Paul wrote, "Likewise the Spirit also helps in our weaknesses, for
we do not know what we should pray for as we ought, but the Spirit
Himself makes intercession for us" (Romans 8:26). What's even
more, the Holy Spirit knows and understands the mind of Christ,
and He will help us pray accordingly.

First Corinthians 2:11–12 says, "For what man knows the things
of a man except the spirit of the man which is in him? Even so we
have received, not the spirit of the world, but the Spirit who is from

God, that we might know the things that have been freely given to us by God." So while we're praying, the Father wants to honor our requests and bless us, but there's a higher calling in prayer. Prayer is a way to ask for things that, when given, will be used exclusively to bring glory to God through His Son—the Lord Jesus Christ!

✧✧✧

Communion with God through His Word and
prayer is as indispensable to us as the natural food we
eat and the necessary air we need to breathe.

 Further reading, meditation, and study—John 14:12–14; James 4:1–3

NEW THINGS

Do not remember the former things, nor consider the
things of old behold I will do a new thing. Now it shall
spring forth; shall you not know it? I will even make
a road in the wilderness and rivers in the desert.
—Isaiah 43:18–19

There are multitudes of Christians who find it challenging to move forward and embrace new things. We humans are creatures of habit and routine. The moment a habit is formed, it can be difficult to break, whether it is good or bad. Isaiah 43:18 says, "Do not remember the former things, nor consider the things of old." Former things are familiar things we were accustomed to doing. Although they may have been good things, that doesn't mean we should continue in them, especially if the Lord is leading us to do something different.

At times, it is great to think about the good times and reminisce about past achievements and victories. However, if we're always thinking about the past and longing to return, we can hinder our progress and our ability to move forward. Some years ago, God was pushing me to shift from the pastoral to the apostolic ministry. I must admit, I had gotten comfortable and familiar with what I was doing. I had formed a pastoral habit, so to speak, but it was time for me to transition and obey God.

When my wife and I surrendered to God's new assignment, I knew it was the right thing. Looking back in hindsight, I realize that had we refused to move forward, we could have missed our season of opportunity. There are multitudes of Christians who miss their seasons of opportunity and purpose, mainly because they feel the past is better than what the future holds. I must admit that early on during my transition, I struggled to discern what God was doing. But I soon realized I needed to trust Him, because He was doing something entirely new in our ministry. (See Proverbs 3:5–6.) My friend, we must make a conscious effort to forget the former things and embrace the new.

✧ ✧ ✧

 Further reading, meditation, and study—Isaiah 43:16–18; Proverbs 3:5–6

DONE EVERYTHING, STAND

Therefore, put on the full armor of God, so that when
the day of evil comes you may be able to stand your
ground, and after you have done everything, to stand.
—Ephesians 6:13 (NIV)

There are circumstances we experience in life that require a response, but there are times when we have done everything to just stand. In Paul's epistle to the believers at Ephesus, he warned them that it's not a matter *if* evil comes, but *when* it comes to stand. The word "stand" means "To take position, set, rest, abide, and endure. It's interesting to note that in spite of everything, including a nearly life-ending experience, Paul chose to stand. One of the ways he chose to stand was by declaring the gospel of Christ in tough situations and harsh environments.

Ephesians 6:19–20 (NIV) says, "Pray also for me, that whenever I open my mouth, words may be given me so that I will fearlessly make known the mystery of the gospel. For which I am an ambassador in chains, pray that I may declare it fearlessly as I should." Please note that he did not ask the believers at Ephesus to pray that his chains be removed or disappear, but instead that he would speak fearlessly and continue to work for the Lord in spite of them.

The devil knows that if he can get believers to come to an abrupt stop and have a pity party, he can defeat us. The trials come to make us strong, not to cause us to fall or defect from the faith. We must stand and keep working. First Corinthians 15:58 (NIV) says, "Therefore, my dear brothers stand firm, let nothing move you. Always give yourselves fully to the work of the Lord, because you know that your labor in the Lord is not in vain." No matter what type of circumstances we experience in our walk with God, we must remain steadfast and immovable.

📖 Further reading, meditation, and study—1 Corinthians 15:57–58; Ephesians 6:13–20

SEVENTY TIMES SEVEN

*Then Peter came to Him [Jesus] and said, Lord how often
shall my brother sin against me, and I forgive him? Up
to seven times? Jesus said to him, I do not say to you,
up to seven times, but up to seventy times seven?*
—Matthew 18:21–22

In Matthew's Gospel, Peter asks Jesus an important question about forgiveness: "Lord how often shall my brother sin against me, and I forgive him? Up to seven times?" (Matthew 18:21). Jesus responds, "I do not say to you, up to seven times, but up to seventy times seven" (v. 22). We should never keep records of the injustices done to us; that is God's job, not ours. (See Deuteronomy 32:34.) God is the Supreme Judge of the universe, and vengeance is reserved for Him only. We must always remind ourselves that God has forgiven us numerous times, and so should we do to those who trespass against us. (See Psalm 78:38.)

So that Peter will gain more understanding about forgiveness, Jesus shares a parable about a certain king who had taken an account of his servants. After the account of his servants was settled, it was found out that one owed him ten thousand talents. (See Matthew 25:23–35.) The talent was the largest of the silver coins during that time. Jesus mentioning that it was a volume of ten thousand shows the enormity of the servant's debt and the impossibility of him being able to clear himself.

Similarly, we, too, had an enormous sin debt and were unable to clear ourselves of guilt, shame, and sin. The atonement of Jesus cancelled our debts at the cross. When God forgives us of our trespasses, we should have compassion and forgive those who have wronged us. We should never seek harm or revenge. The model prayer Jesus taught His disciples includes the phrase "And forgive us our debts as we forgive our debtors" (Matthew 6:12). God honors our prayers when we ask for forgiveness, but he wants us to forgive men their trespasses as well.

✦✦✦

 Further reading, meditation, and study—Matthew 18:21–35; Mark 11:25–26

STRIVING FOR LOVE

And may you have the power to understand, as all God's people
should how wide, how long, how high, and how deep His love
really is. May you experience the love of Christ, though it is so
great you will never full understand it. Then you will be filled
with the fullness of life and power that comes from God.
—Ephesians 3:18–19 (NLT)

There are multitudes of Christians who struggle to comprehend and
experience the Father's love. In an effort to experience His love,
many have become frustrated from constant striving to please Him.
At times they become jealous and critical of those who know and
experience God's love. Throughout Jesus's ministry on earth, He
demonstrated time and time again the Father's compassionate love to
sinners. These were people and outcasts who did not earn it or had
exemplary religious résumés. Many of the religious leaders during
Jesus's time on earth were threatened by His teachings on mercy
and grace.

The Pharisees thought they could earn God's favor through their
own self-righteous works and laws. In fact, this caused them, along
with their contemporaries, to be very judgmental and critical of
Jesus and anyone who responded to His love and compassion. Luke
15:1–2 (NLT) says, "Tax collectors and other notorious sinners often
came to listen to Jesus teach. This made the Pharisees and teachers of
religious law complain that He was associating with such despicable
people—even eating with them."

One major problem with many Christians is a constant striving
for the Father's love. This is often the mentality of many in modern

society who think that if they can get ahead or get on top, it will cause others to accept and love them. This same mindset is often seen in many believers: "If I do more, my pastor will see me; if I do more, God will love me." A preacher once said that love is found in a consistent display of interest, commitment, sacrifice, and attention. This invariably describes God's love for us; His love is unconditional.

✦ ✦ ✦

I was sinking deep in sin, far from the peaceful shore;
Very deeply stained within, sinking to rise no more;
But the Master of the sea heard my despairing cry:
From the waters lifted me, now safe am I.
Love lifted me! When nothing else would help, love lifted me.[13]

 Further reading, meditation, and study—Ephesians 3:14–21; 1 John 3:1–3

TOTAL PROTECTION

Who shall separate us from the love of Christ? Shall tribulation, or distress or persecution, or famine, or nakedness, or peril or sword …Yet in all these things we are more than conquerors through Him who loved us.
—Romans 8:35, 37

There's an array of valuable benefits as a result of our relationship with the Father, and one in particular is total protection. It's not a secret that we live in a corrupt, unpleasant society and the truth is that it's not going to get any better soon. Second Timothy 3:1 says "that perilous times will come." The word "perilous" means "dangerous, unsafe, terrifying and hazardous." We also read further down, in verse 13, "that evil men and imposters will grow worse and worse, deceiving and being deceive." Newspapers and television show young and old people walking into public schools, churches, and college campuses and killing people at random.

Although these horrible things are happening, the Father protects His children. Psalm 91:9 says, "Because you have made the Lord, who is my refuge, even the Most High, your dwelling place. No evil shall befall you, nor shall any plague come near your dwelling." A refuge speaks of a safe haven and protection. An earthy father will go to great lengths to protect His children, but just imagine what our Heavenly Father will do when His children are threatened. Matthew 10:29–31 says, "Are not two sparrows sold for a copper coin? And not one of them falls to the ground apart from your Father's will. But the very hairs of your head are all numbered. Do not fear therefore; you are of more value than many sparrows."

161

Two sparrows sold for a copper coin is equivalent to one penny, yet Jesus says, "not one of them falls to the ground apart from your Father's will." Then He makes this comforting and encouraging statement: "Do not fear therefore; you are of more value than many sparrows." In short, if our Heavenly Father is immensely concerned about birds that seem insignificant in value, just think how He feels about us, as we are fearfully and wonderfully made in His image. Our Heavenly Father will never leave us or forsake us. He will guard and protect us because He really cares about us.

✧✧✧

 Further reading, meditation, and study—Psalm 91:1–16; Romans 8:31–38

AFTER THE STORM

When your heart is lifted up, and you forget the Lord your God who brought you out of the land of Egypt, from the house of bondage ... And you shall remember the Lord your God ...
—Deuteronomy 8:14, 18

One of my favorite gospel groups during the nineties was a female gospel group called Witness. They produced a gospel track entitled "After the Storm Is Over." It's a very beautiful, inspiring song, and it raises an important question we all must ask ourselves: what are we going to do after our storms have passed? Will we quickly forget how God delivered or healed us? Will we go on with our lives as though God never did anything for us? It's no secret that all of us will face spiritual or physical storms of some sort; there's no escaping them. Paul wrote, "We must, through many tribulations, enter the kingdom of God" (Acts 14:22).

The good news is that every type of storm will eventually pass. Many people have been delivered from horrendous storms or trials. Perhaps your spiritual storm has long since passed over you. But while you were going through the storm, you stayed on your face before God and even set aside time to commune and fellowship with Him. But now that your storm has passed, the question remains: what are you going to do? Will you continue to pray and seek God's face? Will you continue to commune and fellowship with Him? Will you continue to worship, honor, and praise Him? Good questions, right?

In the New Testament, there were ten lepers who experienced a storm of health problems (Luke 17:11–19). Leprosy was a serious issue, and these lepers understood the severity of their problems, but there

163

was one who did not forget the Lord who healed him. Verses 15–19 say, "And one of them, when he saw that he was healed, returned and with a loud voice glorified God ... And He [Jesus] said unto him, arise go thy way thy faith made thee whole." In my understanding, he received more than just healing, he got the complete package. So now that your storm is gone, what will you do? Will you continue to seek God's face? Will you pray and worship Him? Will you return like the leper and render thanks to the Lord, who has brought you out with a mighty hand?

✧ ✧ ✧

 Further reading, meditation, and study—Deuteronomy 8:1–20; Luke 17:11–19

DESPISING THE SHAME

The Sovereign Lord God has spoken to me, and I have listened.
I do not rebel or turn away. I give my back to those who beat
me and my cheeks to those who pull out my beard. I do not
hide from shame, for they mock me and spit in my face.
—Isaiah 50:5–6 (NLT)

Shame is very cruel and unpleasant; more than often, it is the result of sexual abuse or being an object of ridicule. There's a great percentage of people, as well as Christians, who are wonderfully filled with the Holy Spirit but still suffer to some degree from shame. It could be that things that happened in their childhood were never brought fully to the cross. Perhaps they were sexually abused by a loved one or close family member.

Some time ago, I read a true story about a woman whose father was a professing Christian. She was sexually abused by him when she was nine years of age. It left her with a tormenting question: "Is there something bad in me that made him do it?" It was only when she came to the cross that she was set free from shame. Yet there is another true story about a young girl who was sexually abused and later gang raped by a group of young boys. She struggled to escape her agonizing, painful past and it brought her great shame as well. Sometime later, she was delivered by having a vision of Jesus naked on the cross and realizing He had suffered much shame and agony. She also realized that Jesus paid the penalty for her shame.

My friend, everything, including the examples I shared as they pertain to shame, have a remedy that is found at the cross. Jesus was naked on the cross for three hours; there was no loincloth as we

a

always see in pictures of Him. His shame was exposed to everyone who passed by, and they mocked Him. Hebrews 12:2 (NLT) says, "We do this by keeping our eyes on Jesus, on whom our faith depends from start to finish. He was willing to die a shameful death on the cross because of the joy He knew would be His afterward." If you have a background you're ashamed of or a past that haunts you and follows you, please remember that Jesus bore your shame completely!

✧✧✧

 Further reading, meditation, and study—Isaiah 50:4–6; 53:3–7; Hebrews 12:1–2

LIBERATED FROM GUILT

All of us have strayed away like sheep. We have left
God's path to follow our own. Yet the Lord laid
on Him [Christ] the guilt and sins of us all.
—Isaiah 53:6 (NLT)

Should we feel guilty when we commit acts of sin? Absolutely, emphatically, yes! A guilty conscience should prompt us to confess and repent. But if we have repented of our sins and Satan brings about feelings of guilt to our minds constantly, that's not a good thing. To put it another way, if we have confessed and repented and have an ongoing sense of guilt, we have not been fully liberated and will struggle to live victorious lives in Christ. (See John 8:32.) God does not want us to have any lingering sense of guilt whatsoever.

For instance, if every time we approach God with faith, having repented of our sins, and Satan reminds us of our past sins and mistakes and causes us to doubt, the Lord will not hear us. Let me explain this in another way. To come to God with boldness is to know we can and have been forgiven. First John 1:9 says, "I we confess our sins He is faithful and just to forgive us our sins and to cleanse us from all righteousness." However, the minute we confess and repent of all our sins and trust God for forgiveness, we must not go on agonizing about sins we have committed in the past. (See 1 John 3:21–22.)

If one has a true sense of guilt, it must be that one has not confessed an area of sin in one's life. (See Psalm 66:18.) Satan's objective is to accuse us and bring about feelings of guilt, but we should never succumb to his deception if we have confessed and forsaken sin. At the cross, a divine exchange was made. Jesus was made sin with our sinfulness so that we might be made righteous with His righteousness. (See 2 Corinthians 5:21.) Once we embrace that fact, Satan can no longer keep us in a perpetual state of guilt. In other words, Satan's main weapon has been taken away from him. (See Revelation 12:11.) We can go on to live victorious lives in Christ.

✧✧✧

 Further reading, meditation, and study—Isaiah 53:1–5; John 8:31–34; 1 John 3:21–22

GOD STILL SPEAKS

I am the good shepherd; and I know My sheep,
and am known by My own ... My sheep hear My
voice, and I know them and they follow me.
—John 10:14, 27

God still speaks and communicates; He's neither mute nor dumb. Contrary to what some believe, He still speaks to His children in this dispensation. The question is, Do we respond to His voice? John 10:27 says, "My sheep hear My voice, and I know them, and they follow Me." Christians are symbolic of sheep and are familiar with the voice of their shepherd. Just like natural sheep that recognize their shepherd, God has a distinct voice that only we know. One defining thing that often got the Israelites in trouble was their inability and failure to heed the voice of God. There were times when He spoke but they either neglected or refused to listen.

Could this be one of the reasons why some Christians miss their season of opportunity and God's best for their lives? Spiritual earwax could possibly be the culprit behind an inability to hear and has left many spiritually deaf or dead. A man walked into his office and noticed a device the size of a dessert plate plugged into the wall, emitting a constant noise. It wasn't a loud noise but a constant noise. Because of the thin walls, it allowed people to hear other conversations. The purpose of the device was to trick the ear so what was being said could not be distinguished. *Very interesting*, I thought when I heard about this. *One kind of noise to cover the sound of another.*

Just think: could this be similar to what we experience every day—various kinds of sounds and noises that block our spiritual ears and prevent us from hearing God's still, small voice. Similarly to the office dilemma, we try things to block out noises but only create different noises. But in order to hear the voice of God, we must tune out all kinds of noises. And to be clear, that we struggle to hear His voice or some don't believe He speaks doesn't negate the fact that He still speaks. "He who has an ear, let him hear what the Spirit says" (Revelation 2:7).

    Further reading, meditation, and study—John 10:14–27; 14:25–26; 16:13

PROCLAIMING THE WORD

Is not My word like fire, declares the Lord, and like a hammer
that breaks a breaks a rock in pieces ... For the word of God is
living and powerful and sharper than any two-edged sword.
—Jeremiah 23:29; Hebrews 4:12

Proclaiming the Word of God has a significant place in spiritual warfare. Many Christians walk in denial or are not aware they're engaged in a spiritual battle of some kind. The spiritual battle is solely between good and evil, the satanic kingdom against God's kingdom and His purposes on earth. It's no secret that every Christian who's a threat to Satan's kingdom regularly finds himself or herself the object of his attacks. Satan is infuriated and knows that we are no longer "... Taken captive by him to do his will" (2 Timothy 2:26). One day we'll see the destruction of his Satanic kingdom. (See Revelation 20:10.)

We should never, under any circumstance, use human strategies and methods to win our battles against the kingdom of darkness. (See 2 Corinthians 10:3–4.) God's weapons are available to us as we fight against Satan's strongholds. One of the weapons He has made available is His Word. It's not enough to know and quote the Word; we must proclaim it. Romans 10:8 says, "The word is near you, in your mouth and in your heart that is the word of faith we preach." When we proclaim or decree God's Word through the power of the Holy Spirit, we demolish strongholds that Satan has put in place. The Word of God is a weapon we must employ against Satan.

It appears that the body of Christ is taking defensive measures against him, which has its place, but very few are putting the devil on the run. Many Christians go through pain and suffering because they fail to utilize one of their primary weapons in Christ—God's Word. Out of all the spiritual armor Paul encourages us to put on, the only offensive weapon is the sword of the Spirit. The sword of the Spirit is the Word of God. Consider the wilderness temptation. How did Jesus respond? He spoke His Father's word: "It is written." (Matthew 4:4). That is a pattern for us to follow if we're going to win the battle in spiritual warfare against the devil.

✧✧✧

 Further reading, meditation, and study—Matthew 4:1–11; Romans 10:8

BLOOD OF THE LAMB

And they overcame him by the blood of the lamb and by the word
of their testimony and they did not love their lives to death.
—Revelation 12:11

What is meant by the phrase "the word of their testimony"? It simply
means we must proclaim, confess, or testify personally as to what
the blood of Christ has done for us. In order for this to become
effective, we must personalize and testify it in all our circumstances.
For instance, we testify that "In Him [Jesus] we have redemption
through His blood, the forgiveness of sins according to the riches of
His grace" (Ephesians 1:7). We testify further that "Much more than
having now been justified by His blood we shall be saved from wrath
through Him [Jesus]" (Romans 5:9 NIV).

The Greek word for "justified" is "*dikaioo*." It means "to
pronounce righteous or declare to be right." In addition, the Bible
records that we are sanctified. Hebrews 13:12 says, "Therefore Jesus
also that He might sanctify the people with His own blood suffered
outside the gate." The word "sanctify" is similar in form to the word
"justify." To "sanctify" means "To make saintly or holy," which also
means "to set apart to God." Once we're set apart to God, we are
no longer under the devil's jurisdiction and domain; we're separated
from him by the blood of Jesus. (See Psalm 107:2.) One of the ways
we apply the blood of Jesus is to smear it over our lives by a spiritual
basin, so to speak.

What that simply means is that we do the same as the children of
Israel executed in Egypt during the Passover, but in a spiritual sense.
The application of the blood of the Israelites in Egypt is symbolic of

our salvation in Christ. Jesus was killed, and His blood was shed (1 Corinthians 5:7). We have to apply the blood of Jesus to the place of our personal needs: spiritual, physical, emotional, financial, familial, business-related, and ministerial. Whatever pressing needs we have, we must get the blood of Jesus out of the spiritual basin, so to speak, and onto the problem and against Satan. The way we accomplish this is by the word of our testimony.

Through the blood of Jesus, I am redeemed out of the hand of the devil. Through the blood of Jesus, all my sins are forgiven. Through the blood of Jesus, I am continually being cleansed from all sin. Through the blood of Jesus, I am justified, made righteous, just as if I'd never sinned. Through the blood of Jesus, I am sanctified, made holy, set apart to God. Through the blood of Jesus, I have boldness to enter into the presence of God. The blood of Jesus cries out continually to God in heaven on my behalf.

KEYS OF THE KINGDOM

And I will give you the keys of the kingdom of heaven, and
whatever you bind on earth will be bound in heaven, and
whatever you loose on earth will be loosed in heaven.
—Matthew 16:19

The birth of Jesus on earth marked a new era and the interruption
of the dominance of Satan. The world was in absolute darkness and
was under Satan's control and power. (See Matthew 4:16.) In the
wilderness temptation, Jesus triumphed over all the devil's enticements
and deceptions, and at the resurrection He defeated Satan's primary
weapon—death. Jesus has complete power and authority over Satan
and his demons. One of the objectives of the gospel of Christ is to
bind the strong man (the devil) to turn people from darkness to light,
from sin to holiness, and from the power of Satan to the power of
God. (See Acts 26:18.)

While on earth, Jesus was on a mission, and one of His assignments
was to bind the strong man, the devil, and his works. (See 1 John 3:8.)
But it's now our responsibility through the Spirit to demonstrate and
show forth the outworking of Christ's victory. (See 2 Corinthians
2:14.) One of the ways to demonstrate Christ's victory as well as
ours is to bind the strong man. How are we going to bind the strong
man? We have been given the keys of the kingdom. (See Matthew
16:19.) In ancient times, a key expressed the idea of authority, power,
or privilege. One of the ways we utilize our spiritual keys is to bind
and loose. (See Matthew 18:18.)

Proclamation, prayer, and confessing the Word are some of the
ways we can use our spiritual keys (authority). With our spiritual

keys, we can bind the forces of darkness, which include but are not limited to divination, voodoo, sickness, witchcraft, sorcery, disease, poverty, untimely deaths, frustration, destruction, Jezebel spirits, discouragement, depression, and so on. By proclaiming, praying, or confessing God's Word, we can receive deliverance and freedom and minister to others. There is no logical or valid reason why we should give in or tolerate the devil's attacks when we have been given the keys of the kingdom.

✧ ✧ ✧

 Further reading, meditation, and study—Matthew 16:17–19; Matthew 18:18–20

BORE OUR SICKNESSES

When evening had come, they brought to Him many
who were demon possessed. And He cast the spirits with
a word, and healed all who were sick. That it might be
fulfilled which was spoken by Isaiah the prophet saying, He
Himself took our infirmities and bore our sicknesses.
—Matthew 8:17

Does Jesus still heal today? Yes, Jesus still heals in this dispensation. However, there are several factors that have hindered the message of divine healing throughout the body of Christ. The first barrier to embracing divine healing is a famine of preaching and teaching that does not accommodate it. In order for people to have faith for their healing or circumstances, their faith must first be elevated. Remember: "Faith comes by hearing, and hearing by the word of God" (Romans 10:17). Another barrier to embracing divine healing is allowing popular opinion to shape our beliefs.

Many Christians struggle with this. Instead of thinking for themselves and embracing God's Word and promises, they accept what everyone else says. In the book of Acts, the Bereans searched the scriptures to confirm what they heard. We should do likewise. Another barrier to divine healing is an atmosphere of spiritual bondages (religious tradition, legalism, dogmatism, ceremonialism, and so on). Second Corinthians 3:17 says, "Now the Lord is the Spirit; and where the Spirit of the Lord is, there is liberty." The word "liberty" means "freedom and emancipation." If there's an atmosphere of bondage, it will stifle the move and smother the fire of the Spirit.

The body of Christ must return to preaching and teaching the whole counsel of God, including divine healing. Now that Christ is seated at the right hand of the Father, He is still moved with compassion for those who are sick and oppressed by the devil. What's more, the word "salvation" involves more than being born again. In fact, the Greek word *"soteria"* speaks of deliverance, preservation, healing, and soundness. These benefits are the result of the atoning work of Christ. Christ went to the cross in spirit, soul, and body to redeem humankind in spirit, soul, and body. He is Jehovah-Rapha—that Lord that heals.

📖 Further reading, meditation, and study—Matthew 8:1–17; 9:1–8; 27–31; Mark 8:22–26

OUR ADVANTAGE

Nevertheless, I tell you the truth. It is to your advantage that I go away for if I do not go away, the Helper [Holy Spirit] will not come to you but if I depart, I will send Him to you.
—John 16:7

Do you know it's to our advantage to embrace the Holy Spirit? Jesus said so; He told the disciples it was to their advantage that He send back the Helper (which is another name given to the Holy Spirit). John 16:7 says, "Nevertheless I tell you the truth. It is to your advantage that I go away … the Helper [Holy Spirit] will not come to you …" The word "advantage" means "to gain, profit, and benefit." Again, it's extremely important and to our advantage to embrace the Holy Spirit. A couple of chapters prior, we see Jesus reason why and how they risk becoming spiritual orphans. John 14:18 says, "I will not leave you orphans I will come to you."

I believe there are multitudes of Christians who are spiritual orphans. Why? Because they rejected the Holy Spirit and left Him completely out of their lives. He is the third person of the Trinity, who administers and executes the power of the Trinity in creation and redemption. It's through Him we come to view and understand the relationship of the Father and Son. (See John 16:14–15.) Additionally, because of the atoning work of Christ, He is the one who brings an individual to new birth and gives spiritual life. (See John 3:5–6; Romans 8:11.) And finally, it's through Him that the Father and Son abide in and with the believer in Christ. (See John 14:16–17.)

What's even more, in heaven, among the Trinity, it seems there's an unwavering love and adoration for the Holy Spirit. For example, at one point the Israelites were wandering through the desert and rebelled against the Holy Spirit. To show you how important He is in heaven and on earth, here's God's response to the Holy Spirit being violated. Isaiah 63:10 says, "But they rebelled and grieved His Holy Spirit, so He [God] turned Himself against them as an enemy, and He fought against them." There are more examples, but my what I need you to understand is how valuable, important, beneficial, helpful, and indispensable He is in the life of the believer.

✦ ✦ ✦

 Further reading, meditation, and study—John 14:12–18; John 16:5–15;

THE COMFORTER

But the Helper [Comforter, the Holy Spirit], whom the
Father will send in My name … Peace I leave with you, My
peace I give to you; not as the world gives do I give. to you.
Let not your heart be troubled, neither let it be afraid.
—John 14:26–27

Prior to Jesus's crucifixion and departure, He often warned, encouraged, and comforted His disciples. This was necessary because it was a period of unrest and persecution, largely because of the religious leaders, such as the Pharisees, scribes, and Sadducees. Jesus knew the disciples would need supernatural help and comfort. (See John 14:26–27.) Likewise, we're living in what Paul described as perilous times. (See 2 Timothy 3:1.) The word "perilous" means "dangerous, unsafe, and hazardous." These words certainly express the times in which we live. The Lord Jesus knew we would need a Comforter or Helper as well.

The first time Jesus referred to the Holy Spirit as the "Comforter" was the night before He was betrayed. This was in response to the sadness and grief of the disciples at knowing He was about to leave. The name "Comforter" in the Greek language is "Paracletes," meaning "One called alongside to help." In natural terms, a *paracletes* is like a defense attorney, an advocate, a helper who will fight your battles. The name "comforter," is also a legal term, but with a broader meaning than counsel for the defense. It refers to any person who helped someone in trouble with the law. So you see, the Holy Spirit dwells in us, counsels us, helps us, and comforts us.

There are very few people we can speak with in confidence and share our personal problems with without them getting tired or judgmental, or spreading all our personal business. The Holy Spirit (Comforter, Paracletes, Helper) will keep our business confidential, and He'll never get tired of us. It is an absolute blessing to know we have His abiding presence living inside of us, assisting us in prayer and helping with our circumstances. Jesus could have said, "I will let all of you handle things on your own," but He chose to send help. Many haven't come to realize how much of a blessing His help is and how He's a very present help in times of need.

✦✦✦

 Further reading, meditation, and study—John14:12–27; Acts 9:31

PRAYING IN THE SPIRIT

Likewise, the Spirit also helps in our weaknesses. For we do not
know what we should pray for as we ought, but the Spirit Himself
makes intercession for us with groaning's which cannot be uttered.
—Romans 8:26

In the New Testament, there are different types of prayers (intercessory
prayers, petitions, and so forth), but praying in the Spirit is a very
effective way of communicating to God. One benefit we have is a
direct hotline to the Father. This is very effective praying as it relates
to edifying and building oneself up. (See 1 Corinthians 14:2, 4; Jude
20.) Many Christians don't realize the importance of praying in the
Holy Spirit, or even what it means to engage in this type of prayer.
If we need to be strengthened, we must pray in the Spirit. Jude 20
says, "But you, beloved building yourselves up on your most holy
faith, praying in the Holy Spirit."

The Holy Spirit knows the mind of Christ and will help us pray
accordingly. John 16:14–15 says, "He will glorify Me, for He will
take of what is Mine and declare it to you. All things that the Father
has are Mine. Therefore, I said that He will take of Mine and declare
it to you." When I'm praying in the Spirit, He always points out what
is important to the Father, instead of my self-centered requests and
petitions. He brings to the forefront the heart of God, His purpose,
and His will. There are times when we simply don't know what
to pray for, how to pray about our circumstances, or even how to
intercede for the needs of others.

While I am praying in the Spirit, my mind is in neutral. I depend
solely on the Holy Spirit, and He helps me as I pray. Sometimes I may

get a word of knowledge about someone's situation or circumstance and pray with accuracy. Romans 8:26 (NLT) says, "And the Holy Spirit helps us in distress. For we don't even know what we should pray for, nor how we should pray, but the Holy Spirit prays for us with groaning's that cannot be expressed in words." We may not fully understand what's being said while we're praying in the Spirit. But because He has your best interest in mind, He's praying on your behalf.

✦✦✦

Praying in the Spirit is effective when we turn away from
the vanity of time and toward the riches of eternity.

 Further reading, meditation, and study—Romans 8:26–27; 1 Corinthians 14:2; Jude 1:20

HEART FAITH

For with the heart a person believes (adheres to, trusts in, and relies on Christ) and so is justified (declared righteous, acceptable to God), and with the mouth he confesses (declares openly and speaks out freely his faith) and confirms [his] salvation.
—Romans 10:10 (AMP)

There are multitudes of people who make a profession of faith in Christ and the Bible, but their faith is only in the realm of the mind, not the heart. They take an intellectual position concerning certain facts, doctrines, and so on. This approach, of course, is not true biblical faith, and it does not produce any vital change in the lives of those who profess it. But on the other hand, faith that stems from the heart produces a definite change in those who profess it, because "with the heart one believes unto righteousness" (Romans 10:10).

My friend, it's one thing to believe with the mind sort of approaching the gospel with theories and ideals relating to intellectual facts, but it's another thing to believe with the heart "into righteousness." This sort of faith produces a life that is transformed with good habits and character. (See 2 Corinthians 5:17.) Faith has an important part in our approaches to God. Hebrews 11:6 says, "But without faith it is impossible to please Him [God] ..." Faith is essential for approaching God and for pleasing God. But there's a negative aspect regarding this truth about faith. According to Romans 14:23, "Whatever is not from faith is sin."

This means that anything we do as it relates to spiritual things, if not based on or acted out in faith, is counted as sin. My friend, we must have true repentance when carrying out spiritual acts, and they must be motivated by true faith. If these acts are not done in sincere faith toward God, they're not acceptable to Him and are nothing less than dead works. (See Hebrews 6:1.) True faith from the heart will always cause us to acknowledge our own limitations. We must trust God in everything from salvation to healing, but we must make sure our faith is heart faith and not intellectual faith.

✧ ✧ ✧

 Further reading, meditation, and study—Romans 10:8–11; 2 Corinthians 5:17–21

VIGILANCE

Be well balance (temperate, sober of mind), be vigilant
and cautious at all times for that enemy of yours, the
devil, roars around like a roaring lion [in fierce hunger]
seeking someone to seize upon and devour.
—1 Peter 5:8 (AMP)

When God commissioned Gideon to battle the Midianite army, it
was an extraordinary mission. He had a task of battling one hundred
thirty-five thousand Midianites with an army of only thirty-two
thousand, but he was told, "The people who are with you are too
many for Me to give the Midianites into their hands ..." (Judges 7:2).
Those who showed signs of fear were instructed to go, leaving Gideon
with only ten thousand. As if those numbers were not insufficient
enough, God said, "The people are still too many" (v. 4). But then
God said something very unusual: "Bring them down to the water;
and I will test them" (v. 4). The test requirement focused on one
important character trait: vigilance.

There's a television show I used to watch called a channel called
National Geographic, which I learned quite a bit from as relates to
vigilance. Take, for instance, the lion, which is perhaps one of the
fiercest of animals. His prey is no match for him. He has a strategy in
which he crouches down and hides from his prey. Different types of
animals may pass, moving vigilantly at lightning speeds, but every so
often there's one who approaches his hiding place that's either weak
or not alert. Similarly, the devil seeks to destroy those who are not
sober, vigilant, and weak. A regular prayer life is essential if we're
going to withstand the assaults and temptations of the devil.

In light of the earlier story about Gideon, I would like to ask some important questions. If God was to assemble an army like that of Gideon today, who would qualify? Would there be some who would give way to fear? Or would there be those who struggle to be alert like the prey of the lion? Although God gets full credit for the destruction of the Midianites, He was looking for vigilant men, and only three hundred of Gideon's army passed the test. The thing we must bear in mind is that we must "Be sober, be vigilant [watchful, attentive, alert, observant]; because your adversary the devil walks about like a roaring lion, seeking whom to devour" (1 Peter 5:8).

 Further reading, meditation, and study—Judges 7:1–20; 1 Peter 5:6–11

RESTITUTION

The thief [Devil] comes only in order to steal [take, rob, rip-off] and kill and destroy. I came that they may have and enjoy life, and have it in abundance (to the full, till it overflows).
—John 10:10 (AMP)

Jesus said the devil only comes to steal; that statement resonates with many. For some, he has stolen everything from finances, peace, joy of salvation, health, stability, and purpose. There's good news, because God is in the business of restitution or restoration. Restitution is an act of being restored—as in a restoration of something to its rightful owner, the restoration of a previous state, an equivalent given for some injury, compensation, recompense, and reimbursement. There's an account in the Old Testament about David and the city of Ziglag. It gives us a paradigm of how the devil steals from God's people. (See 1 Samuel 30:1–4.)

As stated earlier, many people had experiences of the enemy stealing from them. David had one of his own. The Amalekites had invaded the city of Ziglag; taken captive their wives, sons, and daughters; and burned the city. Can you imagine how they must have felt seeing everyone and everything taken when they returned home? At sundry times, in a similar way, this is how trials and circumstances come upon the children of God. First Peter 4:12 (NASB) says, "Beloved do not be surprised at the fiery ordeal among you, which comes upon you for your testing, as though some strange thing were happening to you."

The patriot Job could testify about how the enemy stole from him, but God restored to him double for his trouble. We see a similar outcome for David. the Bible says, "David recovered all that the Amalekites had carried away, and David rescued his two wives" (1 Samuel 30:18). We might be inconvenienced and heartbroken at what the enemy has stolen from us, but God is in the business of restoration and restitution. Just like David, we must cast all our cares upon the Lord and trust that He will give us victory, because pain and suffering may last for a while, but joy and peace will eventually come.

✦ ✦ ✦

 Further reading, meditation, and study—1 Samuel 30:1–26; Job 42:1–10

GRACE TO GET UP

For a righteous man may fall seven times and rise again ...
If we confess our sins He is faithful and just to forgive us our
sins and to cleanse us from all unrighteousness.
—Proverbs 24:16; 1 John 1:9

The Prodigal Son, David, and Peter had at least one thing in common: they had fallen from grace. It's always been God's objective and good pleasure to restore people back to their places in Him. This was one of the primary reasons Jesus went to the cross—to restore humankind back to the Father. God graciously restored the prodigal son, David, and Peter. First, prior to being restored, David had committed adultery with Bathsheba, Uriah's wife (Uriah was under his command and also his neighbor). To make matters worse, he tried to cover his sin by arranging the death of her husband.

After the prophet Nathan confronted him, David knew he needed God's mercy and forgiveness. (See Psalm 51:1–10.) Second, the prodigal son asked for what he assumed belonged to him as the youngest son and left for a far country. Satan's plan to separate and isolate him from those who loved and cared about him was set in full motion. But eventually he came to the end of himself and returned home into the arms of a loving father. (See Luke 15:11–32.) Third, Peter was used powerfully by the Holy Spirit but at times was very outspoken and made a few monumental mistakes. But in spite of his setbacks and failures, Jesus restored him and gave him the grace to get back up again. (See John 21:1–22.)

A bus driver with an excellent driving history was put in for a safe driving award by her school district. Her colleagues even trusted her to drive a busload of them to an award ceremony. But on the way there, she turned a sharp corner and flipped the bus, and everyone was placed in the hospital. No one was seriously injured, but did she receive her award anyway? No, the district didn't operate on the principle of grace. I stated earlier that the Prodigal Son, David, and Peter had one thing in common, but actually they had two things in common. They all had fallen from grace, but with God's mercy and grace, they were able to get back up.

✦✦✦

 Further reading, meditation, and study—Luke 15:11–32; John 21:1–22; 1 John 1:9

REERECTED WALLS

I do not pray for these alone, but also for those who will
believe in Me through their word; that they all may be one,
as You, Father, are in Me, and I in You; that they also may be
one in Us, that the world may believe that You sent Me.
—John 17:20–21

Christianity is not divided into groups (whites, blacks, Hispanics, and
so forth) with an invisible wall separating each one. Jesus died for
all races and classes of people. (See John 3:16.) However, on Sunday
mornings, or any given day, I suspect that the Father is not happy
with the actions and behavior of His children. Some argue that
because some races have cultural differences we should not attend
or worship together. That's not biblical, of course; we should never
meet at church or come together on the basis of racial preferences.
Peter had to learn "that God shows no partiality ..." (Acts 10:34).

Just as Jews and Gentiles are given access to the Father, all
races of people have access through Christ Jesus. (See Romans
5:1–2.) However, the wall of separation that Christ abolished has
been reerected. (See Ephesians 2:14.) It is a wall of religious labels,
denominationalism, and racial division. The wall of racial preference
and doctrinal differences still remains an issue today. Why was it so
important for Jesus go through Samaria, seeing as how the "Jews
had no dealings with Samaritans" (John 4:9)? When He ministered
to the Samaritan woman, He broke the racial divide and prejudices.

Additionally, He gave the body of Christ a blueprint on how to
get past racial preferences and differences. He never discriminated
because of skin color; He was moved because of souls. I believe

the intention of God is that His children come together in unison. Before the crucifixion, Jesus prayed that all of God's people would be as one. John 17:20–21 says, "I do not pray for these alone, but also for those who will believe in Me through their word; that they all may be one, as You, Father, are in Me, and I in You ..." One of the ways the world will believe Jesus was sent is by seeing all of God's children, regardless of race or denomination, come together in harmony and unity.

📖 Further reading, meditation, and study—John 17:2–26; Ephesians 2:14–18

Ordered Steps

Commit your way to the Lord, trust also in Him, and He
shall bring it to pass ... The steps of a good man are ordered
[established] by the Lord and He delights in his way.
—Psalm 37:5, 23

There are certain things God will allow us to do, but ultimately His
purpose and will prevail. Proverbs 16:1, 9 says, "The preparations
[plans] of the heart belong to man, but the answer of the tongue is
from the Lord ... A man's heart plans his way, but the Lord directs
his steps." Prior to the crucifixion, Jesus was in great agony His soul
was sad and deeply grieved. With the weight of the world on His
shoulders, He asked the Father to allow the cup of suffering to pass
but surrendered to His will. Matthew 26:38–39 says, "He went a
little further and fell on His face, and prayed, saying, O my Father,
if it possible, let this cup pass from Me; nevertheless, not as I will,
but as You will."

While I was serving in the military, many wonderful things
happened to me. One of those things was a chance to serve my
country. What's even more, I met my beautiful wife, God healed
and delivered me of cancer, and so on. But prior to being healed and
delivered of cancer, I had planned on retiring from the military. I
thought that after retiring I could use my specialty in the civilian
sector. That was my plan, but unbeknownst to me, God had other
plans. Proverbs 19:21 (AMP) says, "Many plans are in a man's mind,
but it is the Lord's purpose for him that will stand."

My friend, I have come to know that God's plans are far greater
than ours. In today's society, people use different words and phrases to

describe a shift, transition, or change in their lives. Some may use the phrase "I'm rebranding or starting something new." It sounds great, but if we think about it, God is the one that's shifting, transitioning, and rebranding us. We have to stay open to whatever He wants and desires for us. Rather than resign ourselves to fate or wishful thinking, we should fully trust and surrender to God's purpose and will. He orders our steps.

✦ ✦ ✦

 Further reading, meditation, and study—Psalm 37:3–6, 23; Proverbs 16:1, 9; 19:21

Impartation of Love

Beloved, let us love one another, for love is of God; and
everyone who loves is born of God and knows God. He who
does not love does not know God, for God is love…Beloved,
if God so loved us, we also ought to love one another.
—1 John 4:7–8, 11

Christ is the personification, embodiment, and representation of
perfect love. His love is beyond our comprehension and understanding.
Not only is love one of His attributes; it is a vital part of His nature.
While on earth, Christ was always willing to demonstrate love
to everyone, including those who were marginalized. He never
excluded anyone—not even His enemies. Similarly, as believers in
Christ, we have a responsibility to act accordingly. We must freely
minister and share God's love and compassion to others. Those who
have experienced God's love will impart God's love. (See Luke 7:47.)

Love is not for us to stockpile or hoard for ourselves, seeing as
it has been poured out in our hearts by the Holy Spirit. Christians
are called to be channels through which God's love and compassion
flow. Two of my favorite gospel groups during the nineties were
Commissioned and Witness. They had songs, respectively, entitled
"Love Isn't Love Until It's Given Away" and "Love Is an Action
Word." These songs speak volumes to how we should impart God's
love to others.

In John 21:15, Jesus asks Peter an important question: "Simon,
son of Jonah, do you love Me more than these?" He said to Him,
"Yes, Lord; You know that I love You." He said to him, "Feed My
Lambs." Jesus continues to ask the same question two consecutive

times. But notice that Jesus didn't say, "Peter, do you love My sheep or lambs? Then feed My Sheep." Instead He asked, "Peter, do you love Me?" Peter's ministry to the Lord's sheep was to be motivated and provoked by His love for Christ. (See 1 John 5:2.) Likewise, when we truly love the Lord, it will motivate and provoke us to love others.

✦✦✦

 Further reading, meditation, and study—Luke 7:36–50; 1 John 4:7–8, 11

RELIGION OR RELATIONSHIP

*But whatever was to my profit I now consider loss for
the sake of Christ. What is more, I consider everything
a loss compared to the surpassing greatness of knowing
Christ Jesus my Lord, for whose sake I have lost all things.
I consider them rubbish that I may gain Christ.*
—Philippians 3:7–8

The Bible is very clear concerning the atoning work of Jesus. Based
on what we know, He came to save us from our sins, to redeem
us back to the Father, to give us abundant life and eternal life, and
to destroy the works of the devil. This list does not fully exhaust
everything Jesus came to do, but there's one thing He did not come
to do, and that is to make religious people. Paul was a very religious
man prior to his conversion. He had zeal, but his zeal did not come to
him according to knowledge. It's very dangerous to be very religious
while not knowing the Lord. (See Romans 10:2.)

Following Paul's conversion, he came to understand and
appreciate the importance of having a relationship with Christ. He
made this confession: "But what things were gain to me, these I have
counted loss for Christ. Yet indeed I also count all things loss for the
excellence of the knowledge of Christ Jesus my Lord, for whom I
have suffered the loss of all things, and count them as rubbish, that
I may gain Christ" (Philippians 3:7–8). There's a vast difference
between being religious and having a relationship with Christ.

Religion is an organized system of doctrine with an approved
pattern of behavior and a proper form of worship. There are a great
number of religious beliefs that are not the same as being a Christian.

The Christian faith is the only one that has relationship. Religion never changes the heart—the core of the problem. It encourages activities that allow people to look spiritual on the outside. This is why Jesus told Nicodemus, "Unless one is born of water and the Spirit, he cannot enter the kingdom of God" (John 3:5). Are you born again, and do you have a relationship with Jesus? Remember: religion is powerless to restrain the sinful human nature, but a relationship with Christ places you in right standing with the Father and develops godly character.

Further reading, meditation, and study—Romans 10:1–3; Philippians 3:1–11

Different Outlook

... But I come to you in the name of the Lord of hosts, the God of the armies of Israel, whom you defiled ... Then all this assembly shall know that the Lord does not save with sword and spear; for the battle is the Lord's and He will give you into our hands.
—1 Samuel 17:45, 47

In the Valley of Elah, Goliath ridiculed and taunted the armies of Israel, as they were intimidated and greatly afraid. He provoked them relentlessly, challenging anyone who would fight against him, but no one was willing to step forward. Likewise, this is how Satan tries to provoke and intimidate God's people. In fact, Jesus said he does not "come except to steal, and to kill and to destroy ..." (John 10:10). And Peter wrote that we should "be sober, be vigilant; because your adversary the devil walks about like a roaring lion, seeking whom he may devour" (1 Peter 5:8).

According to 1 Samuel 17, when David saw the battle and Goliath taunting the Israelites, he had an entirely different outlook and perspective. This is made clear in verse 26, where he says, "What shall be done for the man who kills this Philistine and takes away the reproach from Israel? For who is this uncircumcised Philistine that he should defy the armies of the living God." There's an obvious distinction and outlook between David and the Israelites. The Israelites walked in total fear and lacked courage, but David had courage and a revelation of God's faithfulness and deliverance.

He knew from all his past experiences that God was able to give him victory. When we're faced with intimidating circumstances, we should go back and look at our spiritual archives and see how

God once delivered us and then forge ahead with confidence in Him. So what giants are you facing today? Are you running in fear, or will you be like David, who triumphed over Goliath, trusting that God will give you courage and victory against everything that comes about in your life? The next time you're faced with a giant of some sort, remember to place your confidence and trust in the Lord, and watch Him give you the victory over your enemies and circumstances.

✦✦✦

 Further reading, meditation, and study—1 Samuel 17:1–47; Acts 27:1–44

New Wine and Old Wineskins

No one put a piece of unshrunk [new] cloth on an old
garment; for the patch pulls away from the garment, and
the tear is made worse. Nor do they put new wine into
old wineskins, or else the wineskins break, the wine is
spilled, and the wineskins are ruined. But they put new
wine into new wineskins, and both are preserved.
—Matthew 9:16–17

The above scripture relates to everyday life and has spiritual
connotations. First, the new cloth and old garment: Jesus didn't
come to patch, repair, or mend the traditional practices of the Jews
or Judaism with its drudgery of rules and regulations. Second, the
analogy of new wine and old wineskins: During Biblical times, wine
was kept in wineskins. Once the new wine fermented, it would
expand, which in turn would stretch the wineskin. After the wine
had aged, the stretched skin would burst if more new wine was
poured into it.

The new wine speaks of the gospel message, and new wineskins
speak of those who embrace the teachings of Jesus. The old wineskins
(religious people) during Jesus's time would not make way for
His teaching (new wine). It was incompatible with their religious
tradition and legalistic doctrines. What's more, they did not have
the capacity to embrace or receive truth. In fact, to this day some
Christians read and preach from the Bible but find ways to reject
or eliminate portions of it. New wine also speaks of a renewing of
mindsets. One of the biggest challenges during Jesus's time on earth
was transitioning people from law to grace and truth.

Contrary to His counterparts, Jesus brought in the gospel (new wine), which eliminated the harsh struggles of following the law to live a victorious Christians life. The old wineskins are content with keeping all the rules and regulations, assuming that doing so places them in right standing with the Lord. But on the contrary, Jesus says we are to come to Him. He wants to give us rest—to take His yoke and learn from Him. The moment we decide to come to Him, we'll find that His yoke is easy and His burden is light.

✧✧✧

 Further reading, meditation, and study—Matthew 9:14–17; Philippians 3:1–16

THE BATTLEFIELD

But thanks be to God, who gives us the victory [making
us conquerors] through our Lord Jesus Christ.
—1 Corinthians 15:58 (AMP)

There's no way we could have known that after becoming born-
again believers in Christ we would become spiritual soldiers, fighting
constant battles with the kingdom of darkness. But the good news
is that we've been given spiritual equipment to defend and fight
against the enemy on the battlefield. Throughout our Christian
experience, spiritual warfare can manifest in our daily lives in a
variety of ways through relational conflict, temptation, persecution,
financial hardships, sicknesses, and so on. From the time the Israelites
left Egypt to the dynasty of King David, there was constant war,
instability, trouble, and enemies on every side.

God was bringing them, as with us, to a place in Him a place of
peace and rest. Nonetheless, they would have to trust and depend on
the Lord as they encountered enemies on various battlefields. When
many of us left Egypt, which speaks of a life of bondage and sin, we
were placed on life's battlefield and began a long journey of fighting
the good fight of faith, as Paul alluded to concerning himself. Second
Timothy 2:3–4 says, "You therefore must endure hardship as a good
soldier of Jesus Christ. No one engaged in warfare entangles himself
with the affairs of this life, that he may please him [Christ] a soldier."

I'm grateful for the time during which I served my country as a
soldier in the US military. During my assignments at various duty
stations, I served under and encountered some great military leaders:
lieutenants, captains, colonels, generals, first sergeants, sergeant

majors, and so on. But none can be compared to our powerful military Commander-in-Chief, Christ Jesus. We can trust Him and follow Him into any battle; it makes no difference where and what it may entail. No matter what the devil's plans are or what he attempts to do, we're more than conquerors through our Lord Jesus Christ.

✧✧✧

 Further reading, meditation, and study—2 Corinthians 10:1–6; 2 Timothy 2:1–4

Prosper in Health

And these signs will follow those who believe; in My
name they will cast out demons; they will speak with
new tongues; they will take up serpents; and if they drink
anything deadly, it will by no means hurt them; they
will lay hands on the sick, and they will recover.
—Mark 16:17–18

To better understand why the healing ministry is a vital part of
the church, we must revisit a time when it wasn't uncommon for
anointed evangelists to preach, teach, and operate in the healing
ministry. They include trailblazers of the healing movement (e.g.,
Oral Roberts, Lester Sumrall, Katheryn Kulhman, John G. Lake, Jack
Coe, A. A. Allen, Maria Woodworth-Etter, Smith Wigglesworth,
the Jeffreys brothers, William Seymour, Reinhard Bonnke). Today
there are only a few remaining (e.g., Benny Hinn, Daniel Kolenda).
Early on, many people embraced the message of healing; it was
similar to when Jesus ministered on earth: "The power of the Lord
was present to heal them" (Luke 5:17).

Fast-forward to today. In the body of Christ, the message of
divine healing has taken a backseat, and to some it's controversial,
rarely taught, and has no place in many churches. There have been
books written with the sole purpose of discrediting the subject or
the men and women who believe and teach it. It's no surprise that
many Christians have developed little or no faith in believing God
for their healing, so instead they tolerate their sicknesses and diseases.
For instance, today there are many unsaved people, but does that

mean Jesus has stopped saving men and women? No Christian would believe that He still saves to the utmost. (See 2 Peter 3:8.)

The Bible says, "No good thing will He withhold from those who walk uprightly" and "All the promises of God in Him is Yes, and in Him Amen" (Psalm 84:11; 2 Corinthians 1:20). Anything that's God's known will revealed in the Bible is ours to claim. Is healing God's will? Absolutely, yes! Not only is God willing that none perish; He's willing that His children walk in complete health as well. John 3:2 says, "Beloved, I pray that you may prosper in all things and be in health, just as your soul prospers." Do you believe that? Does that resonate with you? If so, start believing and taking God at His word.

✦✦✦

 Further reading, meditation, and study—Matthew 8:16–17; 3 John 1:1–4

JESUS THE SAME AND FOREVER

And behold, there was a woman who had a spirit of
infirmity eighteen years, and was bent over and could
in no way raise herself up. But when Jesus saw her, He
called her to Him and said to her, woman, you are loosed
from your infirmity. And He laid His hands on her, and
immediately she was made straight, and glorified.
—Luke 13:11–13

Our heavenly Father is not unconcerned, unsympathetic, unmoved,
uncaring, or uninterested about what happens in our lives and the
lives of the sick and incapacitated. When it came to the unsaved, the
sick, and those who were demon-possessed, Jesus was moved with
enormous compassion. Matthew 14:14 says, "And when Jesus went
out He saw a great multitude; and He was moved with compassion
for them, and healed their sick." The word "compassion" refers to
sympathy, concern, care, and kindness. There was something about
those who were sick, lame, afflicted, and demon-possessed that
moved Jesus to stop what He was doing and do something.

Has that changed in this dispensation? Certainly not! The Bible
says, "Jesus Christ is the same yesterday, today, and forever" (Hebrews
13:8). Think about it; Jesus's ministry on earth was a combination
of preaching, teaching, and healing, all working simultaneously and
in harmony. (See Acts 2:22; 10:38; Hebrews 2:4.) The Lord really
cares about the suffering of His children. To strike a balance, some
sufferings are the result of disobedience, some are allowed for the
trying of our faith, some are the result of chastisement, and some are
the result of demonic attacks. For instance, in the New Testament,

there is a woman who has a spirit of infirmity. (See Luke 13:11–16.) To whom did Jesus attribute the cause of her infirmity? Satan. He had afflicted this woman for eighteen years. I would like to point out that she was a child of God. But unlike many Christians who make excuses and tolerate their sicknesses, notice that Jesus did not make any excuse not to heal her. He said, "So ought not this woman ... be loosed from this bond ...?" (Luke 13:16). We have to really grasp this, because the Lord is full of love, mercy, and compassion, and is willing to heal and deliver His children. But the question is, Do we want to be healed or delivered, do we simply not want to take time to ask, or do we want to make excuses for Him not to heal or deliver us?

✧ ✧ ✧

 Further reading, meditation, and study—Matthew 14:13–21; Hebrews 13:8

His Yoke is Easy

Come to Me, all you who labor and are heavy laden, and I will give you rest. Take My yoke upon you and learn from Me, for I am gentle and lowly in heart, and you will find rest for your souls. For My yoke is easy and My burden is light.
—Matthew 11:28–30

Take note of how Jesus says His "yoke is easy and His burden is light" (v. 30). The word "burden" speaks of a load, weight, responsibility, duty, and obligation. A yoke is a heavy wooden harness that fits over the shoulder or neck of an ox or oxen. It is held in place by wooden or leather fasteners and attached to whatever equipment the oxen are to pull. That is a very vivid description of religious tradition and legalism at its best—a heavy yoke that is placed upon the necks and shoulders of believers that Christ did not put there, fastened by statements like "You can't wear this and you cannot eat that," and so on. (See Colossians 2:20–23.)

For example, in Matthew's account, Jesus gave a gentle invitation to His disciples. What a contrast to religious and legalistic systems that place heavy and unwarranted burdens upon God's people. Jesus simply says that we are to "Come to Him." Unfortunately, there are multitudes of Christians and churches who are weighed down with religious bondage. Jesus is saying to them at this very moment, "My yoke is easy."

Jesus did not come to deliver us from just one form of bondage (sin) so that we could surrender to other forms of spiritual bondage (legalism, religious tradition, formalism, dogmatism, and so forth). Jesus is the embodiment of grace and truth, and to be liberated from sin, religious tradition, and legalism, we must come to Him. We'll never fully be liberated and complete if we are in some sort of spiritual bondage. (See Galatians 5:1, 4.) Jesus doesn't give us freedom to sin, but we're free to follow and serve God. Satan wants God's people to settle for man-made rules and regulations, but Jesus came to give us the abundant life.

✧✧✧

The most liberating feeling we can experience
is arrived at by casting upon
the Lord the weight and burden of what others think of us.

 Further reading, meditation, and study—Matthew 11:28–30; Galatians 5:1–6

NOT RETURN VOID

*So shall My word be that goes forth out of My mouth; it
shall not return to Me void without producing any effect,
useless], but it shall accomplish that which I please and
purpose, and it shall prosper in the thing for which I sent it.
—Isaiah 55:11 (AMP)*

When God's servants are faithfully declaring His Word, it's as though God Himself is speaking. It is a declaration of His will and purpose. All of the promises of God come to fruition in due time, and not one of them fails. (See 1 Kings 8:56.) Similar to the effects of rain causing the earth to produce seed and harvest, the Word of God produces a positive effect in the lives of God's people. Second Timothy 3:16–17 says, "All Scripture is given by inspiration of God, and is profitable for doctrine, for reproof, for correction, for instruction in righteousness, that the man of God may be complete, thoroughly equipped for every good work."

Not only does God's Word go forth, but He's faithful to perform and carry it to fruition. Think of a time when you read or heard a message. Over a period of time, it had a tremendous effect on your life. God used a preacher or someone to sow His Word, and after a while it yielded a peaceable fruit. When the Word of God is planted in one's life, in the fullness of time, something positive transpires. It's similar to what Paul wrote to the believers at Corinth: "I planted, Apollos watered, but God gave the increase" (1 Corinthians 3:6).

What a beautiful promise God gives us concerning His Word. He says, "It shall not return to [Him] void without producing any effect, useless … it shall prosper in the thing for which I sent it"

213

(Isaiah 55:11 AMP, emphasis added). The word "prosper" means "to flourish, thrive, grow, and succeed." My friend, we have strong consolation and assurance that whatever God's intentions are for sending His Word (e.g., spiritual growth, deliverance, health, family, marital relationship, business, and finances) it will prosper, flourish, thrive, grow, and succeed.

 Further reading, meditation, and study—Isaiah 55:8–11; 2 Timothy 3:16–17

Extraordinarily Patient

The Lord does not delay and is not tardy or slow about
what He promises according to some people's conception
of slowness, but He is long-suffering (extraordinarily
patient) toward you, not desiring that any should
perish, but that all should turn to repentance.
—2 Peter 3:9 (AMP)

While I was serving in the military, a fellow soldier shared the
gospel of Christ with me on a Saturday morning. He was a devout
Christian and was very passionate about evangelism. I remember
how uninterested I was while listening to what he had to say. In
subsequent days and months to come, he would knock on my door,
but I would disregard his knocks and persistence. Fortunately for
me, God never gave up on me. Second Peter 3:9 says, "The Lord
is not slack concerning His promise, as some count slackness, but is
longsuffering toward us, not willing that any should perish but that
all should come to repentance."

The grace of God has appeared to all men, and I was definitely
a benefactor of it. (See Titus 3:11.) After failed attempts, the young
man finally gave up. God used two soldier—a pastor and a brother
who was also in the same unit—to share the gospel with me. Just
when I thought I was out of sight and mind, God used these men
to water the seed (Word) the young man had planted in my heart.
Unbeknownst to all three men, it was a spiritual tag team that got
positive results. First Corinthians 3:6 says, "I [Paul] planted, Apollos
watered, but God gave the increase." As a result, I surrendered my
life and received Jesus as my Lord and Savior.

In hindsight, I realize that God had extraordinary patience with me during those times, as with all present-day sinners. Sadly, many Christians give up on them, forgetting how God never gave up on us. While reminiscing one day, I thought about what type of man I would have become and where I would have ended up had God's grace and mercy not prevailed. If you you're unsaved and reading this testimony, it shows that God is patiently waiting on you with open arms. John 1:12 says, "But as many as received Him, to them He gave the right to become children of God, to those who believe in His name." Why not pray the prayer below?

Lord God, thank You for sending Your Son, Jesus, to die for me. I know that without Him I would be separated from You forever. I invite You, Jesus, into my life as my Lord and Savior. Lord Jesus, baptize me with the Holy Spirit so that I can live for You. Now, Lord, help me find a true body of believers that I may grow in grace. Take complete control of my life in the name of Jesus. Amen.

FISHERS OF MEN

And Jesus, walking by the Sea of Galilee, saw two brothers,
Simon called Peter and Andrew his brother, casting a net
into the sea; for they were fisherman. Then He said to
them, follow Me, and I will make you fishers of men.
—Matthew 4:18–19

Evangelizing the lost or unbelievers is one of the most, if not *the*
most, important ministries in the body of Christ. But unfortunately,
in many places believers have lost their compassion, commitment,
and desire to reach the lost. Although the church has flourished in
many areas of ministry, evangelism has seemed to be not as important
and placed at the back of the list. God is greatly concerned about lost
souls; it's definitely one important thing we must all bear in mind.
God gave His only begotten Son, Jesus, to suffer and die in our place.
(See John 3:16; Romans 5:6–10.)

The first thing Jesus said to His disciples was "Follow Me, I will
make you fishers of men" (Matthew 4:19). Many in the body of
Christ think it's only the evangelistic ministry that reaches the lost,
and that's partially true. Sadly, some evangelists don't operate within
their calling, and that alone adds to the dilemma of unreached souls.
What's even more, this helps us understand why Jesus said, "The
harvest truly is plentiful but the laborers are few" (Matthew 9:37–38).
Although we may not have a strong desire as evangelists regarding
evangelism, every Christian has been "… given the ministry of
reconciliation" (2 Corinthians 5:18–20).

After the ascension of Jesus, the apostles truly became fishers of
men. They wasted no time, especially after the day of Pentecost. We

read about Peter ministering the gospel under the power of the Spirit, and as a result, three thousand souls were added to the church. (See Acts 2:1–41.) The body of Christ must return to commitment and passion for reaching lost souls, because our salvation is now nearer than when we first believed. Has the gospel reached every living soul? Certainly not! My fellow Christians, we have a mandate to be fishers of men.

✧ ✧ ✧

 Further reading, meditation, and study—Matthew 4:18–22; 2 Corinthians 5:16–20

NO MEMORY LOSS

So let us seize and hold fast and retain without wavering the
hope we cherish and confess and our acknowledgment of it, for
He Who promised is reliable (sure) and faithful to His word.
—Hebrews 10:23 (AMP)

Humans have short memory spans, but that's not the case with our
Heavenly Father. He has no hearing impairment, no vision or speech
impairment, and no memory loss. Many years can pass, and He'll
remember every single detail or promise He made to you as though
it were made a second ago. Never is there a moment in the Bible
when God cannot recall what He said or promised to His servants.
He has extraordinary memory, and no one can ever question that.

I think it's a great idea to keep a prayer journal or diary of
prophetic messages or promises from God. (See Habakkuk 2:2–3.)
You can always open it and meditate on the things you have recorded
concerning God's promises to you. The Bible says we must "Seize
and hold fast and retain without wavering the hope we cherish and
confess and our acknowledgment of it, for He [God] Who promised
is reliable (sure) and faithful to His word" (Hebrews 10:23 AMP).
People may forget and disappoint you, but that is not so with the
Father; He does not have spiritual amnesia.

Noah was in the ark for an extended period of time, but "God
remembered Noah" (Genesis 8:1). After Noah and the animal
boarded the ark, God could have said, "Hey Noah, you're out of
harm's way. Now take care; you're on your own." But that wasn't the
case. He never forgot about him. The same holds true for us. He'll
never promise us something or place us somewhere and forget us.

Perhaps you're in the hospital, a nursing home, a juvenile detention facility, or a prison and are feeling discouraged and lonely. God has not forgotten you. Whatever place or situation you find yourself in, please bear in mind that the Lord will never leave you or forsake you.

✧ ✧ ✧

 Further reading, meditation, and study—Habakkuk 2:2–3; Hebrews 10:23–24

Soul Blessing

Bless [praise, exalt, extol] the Lord, O my soul; and all that
is within me bless [praise, exalt, extol] His holy name!
—Psalm 103:1

One would assume David challenged others to praise the Lord. But a closer look reveals He's imploring his own soul to bless the Lord. The soul or inward man often has to be stirred in the affairs of spiritual things. (See Colossians 3:2.) Has it ever occurred to you that blessing is a reciprocal act? What I mean is that we often ask God to bless us, but we read frequently about David blessing God. The word "bless" in the above scripture means "an affectionately grateful praise," and "to revere, worship, and exalt." David wasn't just casually blessing the Lord with lip service; it came from the depths of his soul, or his inward man.

Psalm 42:1–2 says, "As a deer pants [longs for] the water brooks, so pants [longs for] my soul for You, O God. My soul thirsts for God, for the living God. When shall I come and appear before God?" Those who genuinely honor God do it from the depths of their souls. When we sincerely love God, our souls will make it known; they will boast in Him. Psalm 34:1–2 says, "I will bless the Lord at all times; His praise shall continually be in my mouth. My soul shall make its boast in the Lord; the humble shall hear of it and be glad."

David was implying that in order for his mouth to praise the Lord, he needed the cooperation of his soul. When I was in the pastorate, I often challenged the congregation to praise God. But in hindsight, I realize that in order to bless the Lord, it had to come from the depths of the soul. When such a blessing is given, it will flow freely through the mouth. In other words, the moment we enter the sanctuary, we'll enter into His gates with thanksgiving and His courts with praise. My friend, when we love God with our souls we never need someone to stir or motivate us to bless the Lord. In fact, someone might try to silence us like David's wife in the Old Testament.

✦✦✦

 Further reading, meditation, and study—Psalm 34:1–3; Psalm 42:1–11

Salt of the Earth

You are the salt of the earth; but if the salt loses its flavor
how shall it be seasoned? It is then good for nothing but
to be thrown out and trampled underfoot by men.
—Matthew 5:13

Every believer has what it takes to affect his or her environment
and the lives of people. Jesus says we're the salt of the earth. Natural
salt is a flavor-enhancing agent to food. The key thing about salt
is its enhancing effect. Most people assume that salt adds flavor to
food. But on the contrary, salt contributes to the release of flavor by
breaking down the cell walls in vegetables, fruits, and meats. As a
result, the natural flavor of the food comes to life. As the cells break
down in vegetables, fruits, or meats, aromas and flavors are released.
Similarly, just as salt is an enhancing agent to food, we must affect
and enhance the world around us.

We have the indwelling of the Spirit empowered to affect others'
lives. On my last day delivering mail at my transfer station, I was
just about ready to go home when the postmaster delivered a speech
about my time there. I was moved by her kind remarks. She asked
if I had something to say. I asked whether I could pray for everyone
there. She said, "Sure." Afterward, I was heading toward my vehicle
when I heard someone say, "Can I speak with you?" I said, "Yes."
It was one of my coworkers. He said, "I've been watching you since
you came here. You are a true man of God." But what really blessed
me was his desire to know more about Jesus. From that moment, he
became a Christian, and we stayed in touch.

Have you noticed how sinners were drawn to Jesus? He brought out the best in them, and as a result, their lives were transformed. A great example of this is the story of Zacchaeus, a rich tax collector. Jesus stopped by his house, and the moment He entered Zacchaeus's life, things drastically changed. He decided to "give half of his goods to the poor and restore fourfold to them who were falsely accused" (Luke 19:8). My friend, because we're the salt of the earth, we're called to effect change and impact the lives of unbelievers. (See Ephesians 5:15–16; Colossians 4:5.) Wherever God places us, we can effect change, uplift, enhance, and glorify our Father in heaven.

✧✧✧

 Further reading, meditation, and study—Ephesians 15–21; Colossians 4:1–6

FAITH TO BE HEALED

And in Lystra a certain man without strength in his feet was sitting a cripple from his mother's womb, who had never walked. This man heard Paul speaking, Paul observing him intently and seeing that he had faith to be healed.
—Acts 14:8–9

A young man years ago asked me a very important question. He said, "How do I get faith to believe God for my breakthrough?" My response was that faith comes by hearing, and hearing by the Word of God. (See Romans 10:17.) In other words, we can acquire faith by hearing or reading the Bible, the Scriptures. In the book of Acts, a crippled man at Lystra had faith to be healed. But I believe that prior to that encounter, his faith was stirred and motivated by hearing the Word of God. We can only speculate what really happened leading up to that point. Hearing, reading, or meditating on the Scriptures will certainly build our faith in an area.

Often when faced with adversity, it seems as though our faith is plummeting and the world around us is falling apart. It's during those times we must make a conscious effort to absorb and meditate on God's Word. The Bible is full of wisdom, spiritual knowledge, and words of faith. For instance, the book of Proverbs encourages us to heed the Word of the Lord, for in doing so "they are life to those who find them, and health to all their flesh" (Proverbs 4:22). I love this scripture because it's not limited to just healing, but we are promised health to our flesh.

The only way we're going to starve unbelief is by feeding on the Word of God. Jesus said, "It is written, man shall not live by bread alone, but by every word that proceeds from the mouth of God" (Matthew 4:4). We need more than physical nourishment; we need spiritual nourishment as well. When ministering the Word of God, you can always discern and detect those who are gravitating to the message. I believe they have spent time with the Father and in His Word. Based on my many experiences, I believe that reading and studying the Bible will help ensure we have the faith necessary to overcome every obstacle and adversity in life.

✧✧✧

 Further reading, meditation, and study—Acts 14:8–10; Romans 10:17

SPIRITUAL METAMORPHOSIS

And I am convinced and sure of this very thing, that He Who begun a good work in you will continue until the day of Jesus Christ [right up to the time of His return] developing [that good work] and perfecting and bringing it to full completion in you.
—Philippians 1:6 AMP

Every believer in Christ has a process he or she must go through. A process is a course of action, a method or means by which something is achieved or attained. God has a well-orchestrated process by which He conforms us to Christ and develops spiritual character within us. An example that best illustrates this is the process and development of a butterfly. A butterfly is one of the most beautiful and colorful insects in the world, but the process by which it comes into being is very demanding and interesting. It goes through four stages of a process called "metamorphosis." Each butterfly goes from an egg to a larva, a cocoon, and finally an adult butterfly.

The Greek word that describes metamorphosis is "transformation," which refers to a change in shape. This process begins with an adult butterfly laying eggs on plants and the plants becoming food for the hatching caterpillars. The next stage is the larva. A larva is also called a caterpillar if the insect is a butterfly or a moth. The job of the caterpillar is to eat and eat and eat. This can speak to the fact that in order to grow spiritually in the Lord, we need plenty of spiritual food, or the Word of God. (See Matthew 4:4.) As the caterpillar grows, it splits its skin and sheds it about four or five times. This can speak to the fact that God prunes us so that we can bear more fruit. (See John 15:2.)

When the caterpillar is fully grown, it encases itself in a chrysalis. Depending on the species, the cocoon may hang under a branch or lie hidden in leaves or buried underground. This process can speak to the fact that God may separate and isolate us to prepare us. As big changes are taking place inside of us, spiritual growth is attained as well. The last stage is when the cocoon becomes a beautiful and colorful adult butterfly. The final stage of the butterfly is similar to the end purpose that God is bringing us to—to mature believers to have the mind of Christ, making them into people who will be able to overcome the adversities and storms of life.

Great growth doesn't come into your life through mountaintop experiences. Great growth comes through the valleys and low places where you feel limited and vulnerable. The time God is really moving in your life may seem to be the lowest moment you have ever experienced. Most believers think that God works when the blessing comes. That's not true! God is working on you your faith and your character, when the blessing is delayed.[14]

NO RETIREMENT PLAN

Now Joshua was old, advanced in years. And the Lord
said to him. You are old, advanced in years, and there
remains very much land yet to be possessed.
—Joshua 13:1

Perhaps God could have said, "Joshua you're advanced in years, and
now it's time for you to retire, get some much needed rest." But no,
He said, "There remains much land yet to be possessed." I believe
this is an encouraging word for many who are advanced in age or feel
they have nothing left in them to give. When we surrendered our
lives to Jesus many years ago, many of us were young, full of zeal, and
driven with purpose. Now, similarly to Joshua, many have become
advanced in years—fifty, sixty, seventy, or even older—and haven't
even begun to make ground. But when the Lord spoke to Joshua in
the above scripture, Joshua was eighty-five years old.

It's important to understand that what matters most is not how
we start something but how we finish. It's not what we can do in
our own strength, but what the Holy Spirit does through us. As
long as we have breath in us, we can do all things through Christ,
who strengthens us, and do exploits in the kingdom of God. When
carrying out the purposes of God, people tend to look at the age of
an individual. The devil may also use that against you by saying,
"You're too young to do this or that" or "Hey, you're too old; you
don't have the strength you once had," and so on.

I was reading a book by the late Kathryn Kulhman and learned
that she didn't start her healing ministry until she was around fifty-
two years old. Although, the late Derek Prince started out as a

pastor, it wasn't until he was fifty-five years old that he stepped into the healing and deliverance ministry. There were others who had similar experiences in the advanced years of their lives. So why am I sharing this with you? Because I believe it's important to understand that when God uses us, we're not restricted by gender, race, or even advancement in years. When we lean not on our own understanding and trust God, we'll complete the work or assignment He has commissioned us to do. Always remember that there's no retirement plan on earth in God.

✦ ✦ ✦

 Further reading, meditation, and study—Joshua 13:1–7; Ruth 4:13–21

LONELINESS EXACERBATED

*And I will pray the Father, and He will give you another
Helper that He may abide with you forever, the Spirit of
truth ... but you know Him, for He dwells with you and will
be in you. I will not leave you orphans I will come to you.*
—John 14:16–18

Towards the end of the year around the holidays people seemed to
be happier and friendlier. It appears that everywhere you go there's
a feeling of excitement and joy that permeate the atmosphere. Sadly
not everyone is experiencing joy, peace and happiness. There are
some who are lonely and depressed perhaps because of the loss of a
love one or living alone. Loneliness is often most poignant during
the holiday season. It seems counterintuitive, but the reason is the
nature of the season.

The holiday season is generally thought of as a time of joy, peace,
and love, but it's also a time when many succumb to loneliness,
despair, and depression. One example of this is someone coping with
the death of a loved one. If the person had no children and his or her
house is empty, when the holidays or the anniversary of the death
of the loved one arrive, loneliness and depression start to creep in. I
was told some time ago by someone who worked for a lady that she
struggled tremendously around the holidays because her husband had
passed away years prior. She would have a very difficult time, often
crying and reliving the experience.

One of the ways the Lord is always near is through the work of
the Holy Spirit or Comforter. John 14:16–18 says, "And I will pray
the Father, and He will give you another Helper, that He may abide

with you forever, the Spirit of truth [Holy Spirit] … I will not leave you orphans I will come to you." An orphan is one who has been left alone because of circumstances beyond his or her control. By having the Holy Spirit indwelling us, we are never left alone. We can commune and fellowship with Him. Second Corinthians 13:14 says, "The grace of the Lord Jesus Christ, and the love of God, and the communion of the Holy Spirit be with you all. Amen." So as you can see, you're never alone; the Lord is always present.

✧✧✧

 Further reading, meditation, and study—John 14:15–18; 2 Timothy 4:9–18

CHANGE IS INEVITABLE

Do not remember the former things, nor consider the
things of old behold, I will do a new thing. Now it shall
spring forth; shall you not know it? I will even make
a road in the wilderness and rivers in the desert.
—Isaiah 43:18–19

Every year, we experience different seasons: spring, summer, fall, and
winter. Each season comes with its own adjustments, transformations,
or changes. The changes that take place for each season prepares an
environment for what transpires in the next season. In life there
will be seasons of change; we can either ignore them or embrace
them. Change is a struggle for some Christians, and especially non-
Christians. But the problem originates in the mind. The moment
the mind is set on something, it becomes resistant to change. What's
more, it will set up defense barriers that will hinder progress,
advancement, and growth.

In some cases, people will sabotage positive changes in their lives
for fear of the unknown. Change is inevitable. What that means
is that it can at times be uncomfortable, difficult to understand,
and hard to embrace. But its unavoidable and inescapable, and if
you challenge people to change, they may become nervous and
uncomfortable. Preaching and teaching about change takes it a step
further; quite often it will provoke people to become angry and
offended. (See Acts 7:1–59.) But change must be embraced in order
to move from glory to glory and from faith to faith.

When Jesus arrived on the scene, He brought about many
necessary changes that were met with opposition and hostility. During

His time on earth, the religious people tried to find reasons to accuse Him falsely. They failed to comprehend that change was necessary and was what they needed the most. The devil hates any positive change in one's life. His agenda is to prevent us from becoming all that the Father would have us to be and to do. We must bear in mind that God has our best interests in mind, and when He begins to shift, transition, and challenge us, we must make the necessary changes. The response should always be trust and obedience.

✧✧✧

 Further reading, meditation, and study—Isaiah 43:16–21; Acts 10:9–16

GRACE OF FORGIVENESS

Therefore, as God's chosen people holy and dearly loved, clothe yourselves with compassion, kindness, humility, gentleness and patience. Bear with each other and forgive whatever grievances you may have against one another. Forgive as the Lord forgave you.
—Colossians 3:12–13 (NIV)

Forgiveness is the cornerstone of our relationship with God and an important part of the gospel message. Given that God has forgiven us through the atonement of Christ, we have an obligation to forgive others. The grace He bestows upon us will birth in us indebtedness, responsibility, and obligation. Jesus placed no limits on the extent to which Christians are to forgive. Luke 17:4 (KJV) says, "And if he trespasses against thee seven times in a day, and seven times in a day turn again to thee, saying, I repent, thou shalt forgive him."

To remain unforgiving shows that we misunderstand the grace of God and that we ourselves deeply need to be forgiven. Conversely, when we have forgiving spirits, it shows we are true followers of Christ. God wants us to imitate Christ's compassionate, forgiving attitude. He forgave those who rejected and persecuted Him. Jesus hung on the cross at a place called Calvary, knowing He did nothing that warranted punishment and death, yet He said, "Father forgive them, for they do not know what they do" (Luke 23:34).

The key to forgiving those who have wronged us is remembering how much God has forgiven us. He is a God of grace and pardon. Daniel 9:9 (KJV) says, "To the Lord our God belong mercies and forgiveness, though we have rebelled against Him." One of the greatest gifts you can give people is the gift of forgiveness. To release an individual from something he or she committed against you will liberate both of you. There are times when Christians disagree, and if God's grace is upon their lives, it should encourage them to be tenderhearted and forgiving. When we are wounded, mistreated, and offended, we must forgive. By doing so, we give the offender the grace of forgiveness.

✧ ✧ ✧

 Further reading, meditation, and study—Colossians 3:12–17; Matthew 18:21–35

ANXIOUS FOR NOTHING

Be anxious for nothing, but in everything by prayer and supplication, with thanksgiving. let your requests be made known to God; and the peace of God, which surpasses all understanding, will guard your hearts and minds through Christ Jesus.
—Philippians 4:6–7

On many occasions, Jesus healed all who were sick and diseased. We can only speculate about what kind of sicknesses and diseases were present during his time. I believe He healed anxiety disorders as well. (See Matthew 8:16–17; 9:35.) I also believe that during Biblical times people experienced various kinds of disorders. For example, take Mary and Martha, who were close friends of Jesus. On one occasion, Mary decided to sit at the feet of Jesus, while Martha was distracted with serving. But "Jesus answered and said to her, Martha, Martha, you are worried and troubled about many things" (Luke 10:41). Anxiety is a disorder having characteristics of worry, trouble, and so on.

It's possible Martha could have struggled with anxiety and Jesus quickly discerned it. Unlike Mary, Jesus recognized that Martha's cares hindered her from fellowship with Him. Martha's mind was weighed down. That's the core of anxiety: worrying about something, such as the future, that you don't have control over. What's more, anxiety often takes place when an individual neglects to pray. Prayerlessness is an open door for negative things to enter in. Philippians 4:6–7 says, "Be anxious for nothing, but in everything by prayer and supplication, with thanksgiving, let your requests be made known to God; and the peace of God, which surpasses all understanding, will guard your hearts and minds through Christ Jesus."

The moment we pray about our problems, we'll experience a peace that surpasses all understanding. You cannot explain it, you cannot put words to it, but peace will guard your heart and mind through Christ Jesus. During wartime, in order to prevent a hostile invasion or keep the inhabitants of a city from being overtaken, there must be a guard or guards. In view of the fact that the mind is sort of a battle zone filled with problems, circumstances, and trials, it needs to be protected by a guard, and that guard is peace through Christ Jesus.

✦✦✦

 Further reading, meditation, and study—Luke 10:38–42; Philippians 4:4–9

MERRY HEART

A merry heart makes a cheerful countenance [face], but by
sorrow of the heart the spirit is broken ... A merry heart does
good like medicine, but a broken spirit dries the bones.
—Proverbs 15:13; 17:22

Depression is a crippling disorder that's prevalent in modern society,
and some believers are no strangers to it. So that we understand how
destructive it can be, here are a few characteristics of those who
have depression: It is a mood disorder that causes persistent feelings
of sadness, emptiness, hopelessness, and loss of interest. It affects
how a person feels, thinks, and behaves and can lead to a variety of
emotional and physiological problems. One of the leading causes of
backsliding is depression. What's more, those who have depression
disorders tend to isolate themselves and become easy prey for the
kingdom of darkness.

It's important to note that in the book of Psalms, David appears
to have bouts of depression. It seems that after he committed adultery
with Bathsheba and arranged the murder of her husband, he became
a very depressed man. His sins overtook him. This is apparent in
Psalm 51:3–10, in which he writes, "My sin is always before me ...
make me hear joy and gladness, that the bones you have broken
may rejoice ... restore to me the joy of Your salvation." These
transgressions depressed David; we know this because he asks God
to restore the joy of His salvation.

There are at least two scriptures in Proverbs that suggest that one
of the antidotes for depression is a merry heart. First Proverbs 15:13
says, "A merry heart makes a cheerful countenance [face], but by

sorrow of the heart the spirit is broken." Second Proverbs 17:22 says, "A merry heart does good like medicine, but a broken spirit dries the bones." From these scriptures alone, we see a pattern formed that points to a cure for depression—a merry heart. And last but not least, at the cross we can find remedies and solutions for everything in life. Jesus said we must cast all our cares on Him. No matter what it is, we can come and release it to Him.

✧ ✧ ✧

 Further reading, meditation, and study—Psalm 30:1–5; Proverbs 15:13

WORSHIP HIM ONLY

Each of you says, I am of Paul or I am of Apollos or I am Cephas or I am of Christ, is Christ divided? Was Paul crucified for you? or were you baptized in the name of Paul?
—1 Corinthians 1:12–13

In the New Testament Paul addresses a serious problem in the body of Christ. At times, Christians tend to place their spiritual leaders in places they should not be in. They worship them instead of having a godly respect for them. I believe that the worship of men is a sin that the devil instigates. He would rather we worship him or someone else other than our Lord Jesus Christ. Remember that he failed miserably at trying to get Jesus to worship him. Matthew 4:10 says, "Then Jesus said to him, away with you, Satan! For it is written, you shall worship the Lord your God, and Him only you shall serve."

To strike a balance here, the Bible says we should "recognize those who labor among us, and are over us in the Lord and admonish us, and to esteem them very highly in love for their works' sake" (1 Thessalonians 5:12–13). However, under no circumstances should we worship a man or woman because of his or her position or title. Paul wrote, "Let no one boast in men" (1 Corinthians 3:21). Looking back at cults throughout history we see at least one commonality: there was no accountability. Their followers simply did anything they said and literally worshipped the ground they walked on.

My friend Jesus has sent back the Holy Spirit to govern the affairs of the church. The Holy Spirit has imparted spiritual gifts that include spiritual discernment. What's more, we have been given safety barriers from the Lord to counteract or prevent occult situations from occurring in the body of Christ. I truly understand what Paul meant by writing, "If then you were raised with Christ, seek those things which are above, where Christ is …" and "Looking unto Jesus the author and finisher of our faith" (Colossians 3:1; Hebrews 12:2). Our worship, praise, focus, and allegiance should never be directed at a man or even a personality, but always to Jesus.

✦ ✦ ✦

 Further reading, meditation, and study—Matthew 4:1–11; 1 Corinthians 1:10–13

BLESSINGS AND CURSES

I call heaven and earth as witnesses today against you that I have set before you life and death, blessings and curses; therefore, chose life that both you and your descendants may live.
—Deuteronomy 30:19

God gives us freedom to choose, and depending on what kind of choices we make, we demonstrate to Him and others what we stand for or against. Most people choose blessings, but due to no fault of their own, they also experience ancestral or generational curses. This is perhaps because of the sinful deeds of ancestral bloodlines: great-grandparents, grandparents, parents, or other close relatives who were involved in the occult or worshipped false gods. I'm not suggesting we receive punishment for sins of our forefathers. But we can expect the outworking or effects that come from their transgressions until someone breaks it off within the family bloodline.

Proverbs 26:2 says, "Like a flitting sparrow, like a flying swallow so a curse without a cause shall not alike." Jesus has made provision for every kind of curse. There are some steps we can take that will release us from generational curses. First, we must confess our faith in Christ and His sacrifice on our behalf. (See Romans 10:9–10.) Confession means saying with our mouths what God has already said in His Word. Second, we must repent of all our rebellion and sins to receive God's mercy and forgiveness. Many people want God's mercy and forgiveness but are unwilling to repent; this is a step you and I cannot afford not to do. Third, we must claim forgiveness for all sins. (See 1 John 1:8–9.)

Fourth, we must forgive everyone who has wronged or hurt

us. This is a barrier to people receiving God's blessings. (See Mark 11:25.) Fifth, we must renounce all contact with any occult or satanic practices in the past and present. This is an area that will invariably block the favor and blessings of God on our lives. (See 2 Corinthians 6:14–16.) Finally, if you feel you may have a generational curse in your family bloodline or personal life, please pray the prayer of deliverance and release below. After you have prayed, render unto God thanks and praise, for whom the Son (Jesus) has set free is free indeed.

Lord Jesus, I believe that you are the Son of God and the only way to God, and that that you died on the cross for my sins and rose again. On the basis of what you did for me, I believe Satan's claims against me are cancelled. So now, Lord Jesus, I surrender my life to you, and on that basis I take my stand against every dark evil force that has entered my life, whether it be through my wrongful acts or the acts of my family or my ancestors. Wherever there's any darkness in my life—any witchcraft or occult activity—Lord, I renounce it now, and in the name of Jesus, I take authority over all these evil forces. I loose myself from them, and I release myself entirely from their power. I drive them from me now in the name of Jesus, and I invite and invoke the Holy Spirit of God to move right in and make my deliverance and liberation fully effectual as only the Spirit of God can do in Jesus's name. Amen!

CHIEF CORNERSTONE

Since God chose you to be the holy people whom he loves, you
must clothe yourselves with tenderhearted mercy, kindness,
humility, gentleness, and patience. You must make allowance
for each other's faults and forgive the person who offends you.
Remember: the Lord forgave you, so you must forgive others.
—Colossians 3:13–14 (NLT)

In this life, we will experience many trials and circumstances as
we enter the kingdom of God. (See Acts 14:22.) Unfortunately, a
great proportion of pain and struggle often comes through fellow
Christians in the church. It's expected when a believer experiences
unpleasant circumstances from unbelievers, but when they come
through a fellow believer in Christ, it is harder to process. Occasionally
believers can harbor unforgiveness, but no matter how many times
we're offended by others, the response should always be the same:
forgiveness.

If anyone tells you forgiveness is a simple and easy process, it's
possible he or she hasn't experienced betrayal, abuse, slander, character
assassination, having a loved one murdered, infidelity, divorce, and
so on. Some may confess either that it was hard to forgive or that
they'll never forgive. But nonetheless, we're instructed in the Bible to
forgive; there are no gray areas and no compromise. Colossians 3:13
(NLT) says, "You must make allowance for each other's faults and
forgive the person who offends you. Remember, the Lord forgave
you, so you must forgive others."

Forgiveness is one of the chief cornerstones of the Christian
faith. Since we have been forgiven so much, we should willingly

forgive those who have wronged us—paying it forward, in a way. Remember what Jesus taught the disciples: "And forgive us our debt, as we forgive our debtors" (Matthew 6:12). When you meditate on that scripture, there's sort of an understanding and agreement you must enter into. Just as the Lord has forgiven us, we must release and forgive those who have wronged us. To allow unforgiveness to exist in our hearts, knowing how much the Father has forgiven us, is a double standard.

✧✧✧

 Further reading, meditation, and study—Psalm 32:1–5; Matthew 9:1–8; Colossians 3:12–17

THOROUGHLY EQUIPPED

All Scripture by inspiration of God, and is profitable for doctrine, for reproof, for correction, for instruction in righteousness, that the man of God may be complete, thoroughly equipped for every good work.
—2 Timothy 3:16–17

I love to use character studies in the Bible as illustrations of what can go wrong and how good can come out of situations. We can learn from many of the countless experiences people endured in the Bible—especially our Lord Jesus. Hebrews 12:2–3 says, "Looking unto Jesus, the author and finisher of our faith, who for the joy that was set before Him endured the cross, despising the shame, and has sat down at the right hand of the throne of God. For consider Him [Jesus] who endured such hostility from sinners against Himself, lest you become weary and discouraged in your souls."

The Bible is full of principles and doctrines that pertain to everyday life issues, such as faith, hope, trials, repentance, forgiveness, and so on. The Bible not only highlights their victories, accomplishments, and achievements, but it is careful to point out their weaknesses and struggles. What's even more, by reading the Bible, we have points of reference, assurance, and hope that if women like Queen Ester and Ruth, and men like Joseph, King David, and Paul, could overcome temptations, adversities, trials, and struggles, we can as well.

These Christians were not superhumans but ordinary people who, with the Lord's empowerment and enablement, did exploits. They lived extraordinary lives. Let's not forget our Lord and Savior, Jesus. He is the blueprint for how we should react to adversities and intimidating circumstances. My friend, God has given us everything that pertains to life and godliness and has equipped us through His Word to overcome the adversities of life. No matter what we may face or the challenges set before us, we can carry out the kingdom's agenda and be victorious in Christ Jesus.

✧ ✧ ✧

 Further reading, meditation, and study—Ephesians 1:3–6; 2 Timothy 3:14–17

SECRETS FAULTS

Who can understand his errors? Cleanse me from secret faults.
Keep back Your servant also from presumptuous [arrogant,
insolent, bold] sins; let them not have dominion over me. Then I
shall be blameless, and I shall be innocent of great transgressions.
—Psalm 19:12–13

Anger, bitterness, and resentment are emotional family members that will poison your relationships and obstruct your spiritual growth and progress if you open the door to them. They are hidden sins of the heart that affect not only sinners but believers in Christ as well. Interestingly enough, many in the body of Christ focus more on the noticeable outwards sins but fail to recognize sins of the heart. Both hidden and outward sins need to be addressed. It's important to note also that sins of the heart not only affect laymen; spiritual leaders struggle with these as well.

In Proverbs, Solomon gives a vivid description of an individual who struggles to control his emotions. He says, "Whoever has no rule over his own spirit, is like a city broken down without walls" (Proverbs 25:28). Consider that imagery for a moment. A broken-down city without walls is a terrible sight to say the least—quite an eyesore. The walls are the focal point in this scripture because in the Old Testament, cities that had no walls were vulnerable and open targets for their enemies. This is precisely one of the reasons God sent Nehemiah to rebuild the walls of Jerusalem, because they were exposed to their enemies.

One of the beautiful things about the gospel of Jesus Christ is the fact there's provision for everything at the cross except blasphemy of the Holy Spirit. Because of the atoning work of Christ and the power of the Holy Spirit, hidden sins of anger, bitterness, unforgiveness, and resentment can be eradicated. It's not God's desire that His children walk around defeated and weighed down with hidden sins of the heart. He wants us to be victorious in Christ Jesus. Are you ready to be delivered? Please come into agreement with the pattern prayer below.

Father, I come to the throne of grace boldly and confess all of my hidden sins. I believe that Jesus died for me and that everything I need is at the foot of the cross. I renounce jealousy, unteachableness, rebellion, self-centeredness, anger, bitterness, and resentment. Lord, help me to be generous, teachable, obedient— one who walks in righteousness and who honors You. I thank You for transforming and renewing my mind and cleansing my heart. I give You praise and honor for delivering me, for whom the Son Jesus sets free is free indeed. I ask all of this in Jesus's name. Amen!

GRIEVING FRIEND

And do not grieve the Holy Spirit of God, by whom you were
sealed for the day of redemption, let all bitterness, wrath, anger,
clamor [loud quarreling] and evil speaking be put away from
you, with all malice, and be kind to one, another, tenderhearted,
forgiving one another, even as God in Christ forgave you.
—Ephesians 4:30–32

In the above scripture, we see a connection between the wrong usage
of the tongue and the grieving of the Holy Spirit. Many people are
surprised to know the Holy Spirit has emotions. Remember: He is
the third person of the Trinity. It seems that out of all the members
of the Godhead, He is the one that heaven is concerned about the
most. (See Isaiah 63:9–10; Matthew 12:31–32.) What's more, He's not
an it, a thing, or a force, He's a person that can be lied to, grieved,
insulted, and quenched. What would offend and grieve Him? For
the answer to this, let's look at the verses before and after verse 30:
"Do not grieve the Holy Spirit."

In verse 29, Paul says, "Let no corrupt word [some translations
read "corrupt communication"] proceed out of your mouth, but
what is good for necessary edification." And in verse 31, Paul writes,
"Let all bitterness, wrath, anger, clamor [screaming, yelling, loud
quarreling], and evil speaking be put away from you with all malice."
These negative characteristics point to the wrong usage of the mouth
and tongue—areas many Christians fail to recognize as violating
the Holy Spirit. It's important to note that Paul was not writing to
unbelievers; in fact, these were Christians located at the church of
Ephesus.

For instance, an acceptable absence from church, missing a few days of Bible study, failure to give offerings, or forgetting to speak to the pastor and his wife are not reasons the Holy Spirit is grieved. Although those things can be considered borderline bad things for some and happen to the best of Christians, in my understanding the Holy Spirit is grieved when our tongues are not yielded and surrendered to Him. Those of us who are born again must be mindful that our bodies—and that includes our tongues—are the temple of the Holy Spirit. We must make sure we never grieve our Friend.

✧ ✧ ✧

 Further reading, meditation, and study—Ephesians 4:25–32; Matthew 12:31–32

LOVE IN ACTION

And He went to the Pharisee's house, and sat down to eat.
And behold, a woman in the city who was a sinner, when
she knew that Jesus sat at the table in the Pharisee's house,
brought an alabaster flask of fragrant oil, and stood at His
feet behind Him weeping; and she began to wash His feet
with her tears, and wiped them with the hair of her head; and
she kissed His feet and anointed them with fragrant oil.
—Luke 7:36–38

Have you ever tried to repay someone who blessed you in some
way? How can you show someone love and gratitude for an act of
kindness that's beyond payment? Just ask Mary, the sister of Martha,
and Lazarus, who showed up at a Pharisee's house unannounced.
Somehow Mary knew that Jesus would be there at a certain time.
What's more, she did not come empty-handed, for she had a purpose
in mind to bless the one who had done so much for her. God had
delivered her from many sins, and similar to one of the ten lepers
Jesus had healed, she returned to thank Him.

It's worth noting that many Bible scholars believe the woman
mentioned here is possibly Mary, Lazarus and Martha's sister. I
tend to concur with their assessment, because in every place she's
mentioned we're given the impression that Mary sincerely loved Jesus
with all her heart. For instance, this is also seen when she and Martha
encounter Jesus when their brother dies and is brought back to life.
Notice in that account how Mary was captivated by what Jesus had
to say rather than by what He could do for her. (See Luke 10:38–42.)

This really caught my attention—especially in a time when there's self-centeredness. Mary put her love for Jesus into action.

Consider how throughout the Gospels, many reach out to touch Jesus and even search for Him, but very few are interested in what He has to say. Jesus is very much aware of their motives. (See John 2:24.) One of my favorite gospel groups, Commissioned, has a great track with the lyrics "Love isn't love until it's given away." A song writer once said that love is an action word. In other words, it's not merely lip service but originates from the heart and is put into action. The Lord Jesus knows the difference between those who love with their mouths and those who love with their hearts.

There are many ways to love and help people, but the most effective way is to pray for them.

📖 Further reading, meditation, and study—Luke 7:36–50; Luke 9:10–17

MOVED WITH COMPASSION

Then Jesus, moved with compassion, stretched out His
hand and touched him, and said to him, I am willing;
be cleansed. As soon as He had spoken, immediately
the leprosy left him, and he was cleansed.
—Mark 1:41–42

People who are moved with compassion don't just stare with unconcern at the heartbroken sufferer. They're people who are moved to do something about their circumstances. For instance, the Good Samaritan encountered a wounded victim in his path, but unlike the unsympathetic and uncompassionate priest and Levite who passed on the other side, he was moved with compassion to do something. Luke 10:34 (KJV) says, "And he went to him, and bound up his wounds, pouring in oil and wine, and set him on his own beast, and brought him to an inn, and took care of him."

Jesus acted in a similar way with a leper as soon as He came in contact with him "He was moved with compassion, [He] put forth His hand and touched him" (Mark 1:41). It's important to point out that by Jesus touching him was extremely remarkable within itself. Everyone knew that leprosy was highly contagious and required the victim to be quarantined. But Jesus was not limited by health protocols, regulations, and precautions. All He knew was that the man needed assistance, and He was willing to administer healing.

Perhaps your situation is entirely different. You may be battling some other type of contagious deadly disease. But regardless of what you're enduring at this present moment, just know that the Lord is moved with compassion. Just consider the two blind men sitting by the wayside. The Bible records that "Jesus stood still and called them … had compassion on them and touched their eyes" (Matthew 20:32–34). What you and I understand is that the Lord is no respecter of persons. What Jesus did for the multitudes throughout the Bible He's willing to do for us.

✦✦✦

 Further reading, meditation, and study—Mark 1:40–45; Luke 10:25–37

RIGHTEOUSNESS THAT EXCEEDS

For I bear them witness that they have a zeal for God, but not according to knowledge. For they being ignorant of God's righteousness, and seeking to establish their own righteousness, have not submitted to the righteousness of God, for Christ is the end of the law for righteousness to everyone who believes.
—Romans 10:1–4

One important thing we must come to terms with is that God has accepted the righteousness only of His Son, Jesus, who has never known sin. What's more, God will accept only righteousness that surpasses the religious leaders of Jesus's time on earth. Matthew 5:20 says, "For I say to you, that unless your righteousness exceeds the righteousness of the scribes and Pharisees, you will by no means enter the kingdom of heaven." Why was it so important for Jesus to point out these two religious sects, the Pharisees and scribes? One reason is that the Pharisees had a strong commitment to observing the law of God, but it was the scribes who applied and interpreted it for them.

Additionally, during Jesus's time on the earth, many of the priests had defected from the faith, so it was natural for the Pharisees to look to the scribes, who were experts in the law. However, Jesus discerned the hearts of these religious leaders. Although they carefully observed the law as far as appearances go, their hearts were far from Him. It's important for us to understand that God is interested not just in what we do but also in our motives for doing it. (See James 4:1–3.) Our motives have to be pure and Christ-centered. The Pharisees failed miserably in this area because they loved the attention and praise of men more than God. (See Matthew 6:1–5, 16; 23:5–7.)

As Christians, we must guard against anything that nullifies the righteousness which comes only from Christ. (See Philippians 3:9.) To counteract the urge to become self-sufficient or self-righteous, or to follow the pattern of the Pharisees, we must put on Christ. We must always bear in mind that our righteousness comes from God. (See Isaiah 54:17.) One reason it's so important to grasp is because "all our righteousness are like filthy rags ..." (Isaiah 64:6). And because our righteousness is stained and tainted, we should stay clear of self-righteousness and embrace Christ-righteousness.

✦ ✦ ✦

 Further reading, meditation, and study—Matthew 5:17–20; Romans 10:1–4

SUPERNATURAL ATTESTATION

*So he went down and dipped seven times
in the Jordan, according to the
saying of the man of God; and his flesh was restored like the flesh
of a little child, and he was clean.*
—2 Kings 5:14

I can recall some years ago going through a very challenging time concerning my health. Two doctors had offered their opinions and expertise about what they expected and thought would be my outcome. But instead I chose deliberately to believe what the Word of God promised concerning divine healing. I was holding fast to the confession of my hope without wavering, because I understood God is faithful. (See Hebrews 10:23.) To strengthen my faith and confirm my convictions, I had a dream about being healed. I can joyfully say that God healed and delivered me.

Dr. Brewton, a great man of God and also a friend, said, "Facts don't change the Word of God; the Word of God changes the facts." Psalm 119:89 says, "Forever, O Lord, Your word is settled in heaven." Every Spirit filled believer has the right to believe and expect that God will supernaturally attest to His purpose and will when we obey Him in faith. For instance, when the prophet Elisha told Naaman (a leper) to dip seven times in the Jordan River, at that moment he had every right to believe the Word of God from the man of God. As a result of his obedience, he received a supernatural healing. (See 2 Kings 5:1–14.)

Jesus is still healing and delivering people in this dispensation no matter what the skeptics and critics have said about the subject of divine healing. Personally, I believe and know this because God healed me of cancer many years ago. God is no respecter of persons. Peter "Opened his mouth and said, in truth I perceive that God shows no partiality ..." (Acts 10:34). If the Lord healed Naaman and men and women in the Bible, He can heal and deliver you and your loved ones as well. Nothing has changed concerning the Lord's willingness to supernaturally attest to His purpose and will.

📖   Further reading, meditation, and study—2 Kings 5:1–14; Mark 16:14–18

LIBERATED FROM
CONDEMNATION AND GUILT

There is therefore now no condemnation to those who are
in Christ Jesus who do not walk according to the flesh, but
according to the Spirit...For those who live according to
the flesh set their minds on the things of the flesh, but those
who live according to the Spirit, the things of the Spirit.
—Romans 8:1, 5

Condemnation and guilt are among things that will hinder Christians
from being victorious in Christ. The devil uses these to push for a
guilty verdict in the courts of heaven. Remember that he is the
accuser of the brethren. An accuser is a talebearer—one who make
up lies and stories about someone. The devil is always accusing
Christians before God. (See Revelation 12:10.) One day he'll be cast
down and destroyed, but until then we must be sober and vigilant
against his tactics and deceptions. Many Christians are unaware of
how condemnation and guilt can affect one's life and rob one of joy
and peace.

The distinction between condemnation and conviction is that
condemnation is used to blame, criticize, and pronounce a sentence.
While conviction is important to bring about repentance and change,
it is the supernatural work and effect of the Holy Spirit. There are
two spiritual agents working to bring conviction to an individual.
First is the preaching, teaching, reading, and hearing of the Word of
God. (See 2 Timothy 3:16–17.) Second is the work of the Holy Spirit.
(See John 16:8.) No one should ever feel condemned after hearing the

gospel of Christ, but what they should have and feel is conviction. (See Acts 2:36–37.)

The meaning of conviction should never be confused with a feeling of remorse and shame, which are words associated with guilt. Should an individual feel guilty that he or she committed sin? The answer is emphatically yes! A guilty conscience should prompt a person to confess and repent. It's only then that we're guaranteed God's mercy and grace and are released from condemnation and guilt. (See 1 John 1:8–9.) What's more, the minute we confess and repent of our sins, the devil can no longer make us feel condemned and guilty. We overcome him by the blood of the lamb and by the words of our testimony. (See Revelation 12:10.) Jesus came to set every captive free.

✧ ✧ ✧

 Further reading, meditation, and study—John 8:31–36; Romans 8:1–5; 1 John 1:8–9

ASKING, SEEKING, AND KNOCKING

Ask and it will be given to you; seek and you will find; knock
and it will be opened to you. For everyone who asks receives, and
he who seeks finds, and to him who knocks it will be opened.
—Matthew 7:7–8

The opposite of people who are persistent are those who easily give
up or quit. Unfortunately, there are many Christians who fall under
that category. They hold up a white flag before the fight even starts.
They make excuses for why they stop short of believing God. Many
of us Christians had that same tenacity and persistence when we
were children or adolescents. If we needed something, we weren't
reluctant and did not hesitate to ask our earthly parents. We knew
our persistence would pay huge dividends. Similarly to how our
parents would help us, God will not withhold anything that's good
from His children. (See Psalm 84:11.)

I'm reminded of a story in the New Testament that Jesus shared
with His disciples about a friend that showed up at midnight needing
three loaves of bread. A mutual friend had come to visit him. But
notice the response and reaction of this man after his friend refuses
to rise from his bed. Luke 11:8 says, "I say to you, though he will
not rise and give to him because he is his friend, yet because of his
persistence he will rise and give him as many as he needs." What if
his friend had given up or said, "What's the use?" He would have had
nothing to set before his guest. But instead he was very persistent.
When believing God for something, it's easy to give in or give up.
But to receive our breakthroughs often requires faith, persistence,
and determination.

Jesus shared a story about a widow that had an adversary that was making her life very difficult. (See Luke 18:1–8.) Every day, she came asking the same question: "Get justice for me from my adversary" (v. 3). As a result of her continual coming, the unjust judge gave in. The key to that story is found in verse 7: "Shall God not avenge His own elect who cry out day and night to Him, though He bears longs with them." We should never be afraid of asking God for help. We're encouraged to "Come boldly to the throne of grace, that we may obtain mercy and find grace in time of need" (Hebrews 4:16). Many Christians become frustrated when their prayers are delayed, but unbeknownst to them their breakthroughs could be just around the corner if only they stay persistent in prayer.

Further reading, meditation, and study—Matthew 7:7–12; Luke 18:1–8

PHARISAISM
(SELF-RIGHTEOUSNESS)

Also He [Jesus] spoke this parable to some who trusted
in themselves that they were righteous, and despised
others ... The Pharisee stood and prayed thus with
himself, God, I thank You that I am not like other men—
extortioners, unjust adulterers, or even as this tax collector.
—Luke 18:9, 11

The Pharisees had many issues they weren't willing to correct. One thing that clearly identified them was their self-righteousness. I believe self-righteousness is among the top hidden sins in the church. Here's why I came to that conclusion. If you look closely at the Pharisees, Sadducees, or religious leaders during Jesus's time on earth, you'll discover that self-righteous people are prideful, arrogant, judgmental, critical, and unteachable. They display an outward show of righteousness, a form of godliness, being overly talkative and very legalistic. In addition, they lack mercy, longsuffering, kindness, and the spirit of gentleness.

Similarly to many Christians and churches today, the Pharisees thought they could match God's standards by keeping all their outward rules. Luke 18:9 says, "They trusted in themselves that they were righteous." This is often the case with religious people who think God's will is the same thing as their itemized list of what they can and cannot do. The Bible says, "They trusted in themselves." To place trust in the flesh or even humans is a disaster waiting to happen. Self-righteousness nullifies the atoning work of Jesus at the cross because the hearts of those who partake of it depart from the

Lord. (See Jeremiah 17:5–6.) Our righteousness comes as a result of Jesus's atoning work at the cross. (See 2 Corinthians 5:21.)

Jesus said something I believe is very important for every Christians as it relates to trusting God and avoiding self-righteousness. He said, "Whoever humbles himself as this little child is the greatest in the kingdom of heaven" (Matthew 18:4). Here are a few things children do that prove they're very dependent. They do not trust themselves in themselves—at least not intentionally. They wholeheartedly depend on their parents for everything. And finally, they have an inner confidence that their needs will always be met. Likewise, this is how we must approach God—as children of God who refuse to rely on or place trust in ourselves, instead relying on or trusting in Him.

📖   Further reading, meditation, and study—Jeremiah 17:5–8; Luke 18:9–14

LEAVING ELEMENTARY PRINCIPLES

Therefore, leaving the discussion of the elementary principles of Christ let us go on to perfection, not laying again the foundation of repentance from dead works and of faith toward God, of the doctrine of baptisms, of laying on of hands of resurrection of the dead, and of eternal judgment.
—Hebrews 6:1–2

Some argue that the writer of Hebrews is Paul. I concur, but that's beside the point. The writer says it's time to grow up and move forward toward bigger and deeper spiritual things. It's important to note that leaving something doesn't always suggest you're forgetting it, but we must never park and stay there. What's more, the writer gives us a list of foundational principles laid at the beginning of our salvation. Remember: these steps are not done later, because this is precisely the dilemma Paul and many modern church leaders found themselves with—church members who refused to leave the milk and go on to the meat of the Word.

As Christians, we'll never get around to building upon the foundation if we lay it over and over and over again. For instance, have you ever driven by an undeveloped property with a foundation that has nothing constructed on it? It appears that the property owner may have had good intentions but never got around to finishing the project. In fact, because the foundation has sat there many years, eventually he'll have to tear it down and rebuild again. In the New Testament, Paul tells the believers at Corinth that he "Could not speak to you as to spiritual people but as to carnal, as to babes in

Christ" (1 Corinthians 3:1). Paul's desire was to take them deeper into spiritual things, but they weren't able to advance.

I can recall that many years ago I was invited to speak at a church. Anytime I'm called to minister, I make it a priority to pray for guidance and the message. As the time drew near for me to minister, I had a dream about the members and its leaders drinking from gigantic milk bottles. Upon waking, I thought about what Paul wrote to the Corinthian believers: "For until now you were not able to receive" (1 Corinthians 3:2). If we want to leave the elementary teachings of the Word, we must avoid envy, strife, division, the worship of men, and so on. As part of growing spiritually in grace, we must choose to walk in Spirit so that we no longer give into the lust of the flesh.

✧ ✧ ✧

 Further reading, meditation, and study—1 Corinthians 3:1–4; Hebrews 6:1–8

BOSOM OF FOOLS

And do not grieve the Holy Spirit of God, by whom you
were sealed for the day of redemption. Let all bitterness,
wrath, anger, clamor and evil speaking be put away from you,
with all malice. And be kind to one another, tenderhearted,
forgiving one another, even as God in Christ forgave you.
—Ephesians 4:30–32

One particular sin that crouches at the door of people is the spirit of
anger. We're warned in the Bible to resist becoming angry because it
"rests in the bosom of fools" (Ecclesiastes 7:9). Is it just my observation,
or does it seem there are many angry and frustrated people in society?
You may experience the anger and impatience of people at a traffic
light once it turns green. If you pull away slowly, you might hear
someone blowing his or her horn repeatedly. The term for this is
"road rage." I was told by a man who lived in a heavily populated
city to be careful how I interacted with people. He said try to avoid
using eye contact if possible when looking in someone's direction,
because it might be seen as an act of demeaning or intimidation.

At the time, I didn't quite understand, because I live in the South,
where everyone, for the most part, seems friendly and hospitable.
However, some years later I would have to act on the gentleman's
advice. My wife and I were picking up one of my sons from college
and I mistakenly pulled into the wrong lane when approaching a gas
station. A young man was driving toward me, screaming profanity
out the window and pointing his finger at me. I could see his facial
expression filled with anger and wrath. I simply ignored him,
looking the other way, and kept driving. By the way he was acting,

it is possible that had I entertained his madness, things might have gotten out of hand. Proverbs 26:4 says, "Answer not a fool according to his folly lest you also be like him."

Throughout our walk with God, there may be times when we become angry, but we're told, "Be angry and do not sin, do not let the sun go down on your wrath, nor give place to the devil" (Ephesians 4:26–27). Similar to Cain in the Old Testament, people who quickly become angry are difficult to reason with. Their anger causes them to make reckless decisions and then have to live with regrets. One of the fruits of the Spirit is temperance, or self-control, which is a very important spiritual fruit that must be exercised to avoid the spirit of anger. If there's a justifiable reason for becoming angry, we should imitate Jesus, who did everything from a standpoint of love, compassion, forgiveness, longsuffering, and righteousness.

Further reading, meditation, and study—Ecclesiastes 7:8–10; Ephesians 4:25–32

ROOT PROBLEMS

And as for what fell among the thorns, these are [the people] who
hear but as they go on their way they are choked and suffocated
with the anxieties and cares and riches and pleasures of life, and
their fruit does not ripen (come to maturity and perfection).
—Luke 8:14 (AMP)

Sin often originates with a root that grows and develops into many
branches. Have you ever tried getting rid of annoying vines or weeds
in your garden bed? I struggled at first trying to remove the weeds,
but the toil taught me a valuable lesson. After much hard exertion
cutting vines and weeds to the ground, they would return with a
vengeance. Not only did they come back, but they grew wider and
taller. The lesson I learned was that clipping or cutting them to the
ground was not sufficient; only pulling them up by the root would
destroy them. So one day I dug up the roots, and I had no more
problems with them returning again.

Similarly, if believers do not kill the roots of their sin, they
will grow into widespread problems. Following is a list of roots, or
problems, that can strangle the progress of believers in Christ. This
list does not fully list all spiritual roots that one can have.

- the love of money
- bitterness
- rejection
- contention
- fear
- unbelief

- self-righteousness
- anger
- jealousy
- sexual perversion
- occult activity
- cares of life

If these roots are never destroyed, at some point God may have to cut them down. Matthew 3:10 (NIV) says, "The ax is already at the root of the trees, and every tree that does not produce good fruit will be cut down and thrown into the fire."

The message of the cross has not changed since the New Testament. God still holds people accountable for sin and unproductive lives. Unproductive lives are the byproduct of negative roots that have sprung up over a period of time. A productive Christian is one who walks in obedience, applies God's Word, resists temptations, actively serves, and shares his or her faith in Christ. But if we tolerate negative roots in our lives, we never live victoriously in Christ. 1 John 1:9 says, "If we confess our sins, He is faithful and just to forgive us our sins and to cleanse us from all unrighteousness." In summary, the thing we must bear in mind is that removing or destroying negative roots will free us and allow us to become all that God the Father wants us to be and to do.

✧✧✧

 Further reading, meditation, and study—Matthew 3:1–12; Luke 8:4–15

Better Covenant

And for this reason He is the mediator of the new covenant,
by means of death, for the redemption of the transgressions
under the first covenant that those who are called may
receive the promise of the eternal inheritance.
—Hebrews 9:15

Covenant is a vital part of our relationship with Christ. Not fully understanding our covenant rights will cause us to forfeit certain rights and benefits. However, this is not just limited to our relationship with Christ but is found in other relationships as well. There are essentially three important covenant relationships: God and His children, husband and wife, and fellow believers in Christ. The root meaning of "covenant" comes from the Hebrew word "*B'rit*," which means "to bind," or "binding." The Greek word for the word "covenant" is "*Diatheke*," which means "to set forth specific terms and conditions." So when we place the Hebrew and Greek terms together, it means a binding that sets forth terms and conditions.

In addition, covenant is only valid through physical death or sacrificial death (dying to self). It's impossible to be in a covenant and remain self-centered. (See Hebrews 9:16.) To make a covenant in the eyes of God is not a ritual; it is a solemn and sacred commitment. Throughout the Bible, each party had to make good on his or her commitment. When God enters into a covenant, there's no more He will do to commit Himself; the covenant represents a final, irrevocable commitment. For instance, when God made a covenant with Abram, He no longer spoke in the future tense. He did not say,

"I will give"; He said, "I have given." In other words, the covenant is settled. It is final and forever. (See Genesis 15:1–20; 17:1–27.)

Covenant has great implication in the life of a Christian, and our comprehending it means we're acquainted with all our spiritual rights and blessings. What's even more, the new covenant God has made with the church is not based upon the sacrifice of animals but on the atoning death of Jesus Christ, the Son of God. (See Hebrews 9:11–15.) This covenant is the one into which all races, ethnic groups, and backgrounds that have acknowledged Jesus as Savior and Lord have entered into. Jesus's last words on the cross had great implications. He said, "It's finished" (John 19:30). The cross is a finished work, with Christ perfecting a new and better covenant.

✦ ✦ ✦

 Further reading, meditation, and study—2 Corinthians 3:7–17; Hebrews 9:11–15

FAVOR WITH PURPOSE

A good man obtains favor from the Lord. But a man of wicked intentions He will condemn ... Now God had brought Daniel into favor and goodwill of the chief of the eunuchs.
—Proverbs 12:2; Daniel 1:9

Sometime years ago, I heard a preacher say that favor isn't fair. Those who don't understand the nature of it will definitely feel a certain way toward you. They will even begin to dislike you for no apparent reason. This often happens once you share how God is favoring or blessing you. Unfortunately, you'll find out how cynical and sarcastic people can be. You might even hear things like "What makes you so special?" "Who do you think you are?" and so on. Animosity directed toward the recipient of God's favor is often the result of a misunderstanding related to not recognizing that the favor of God has divine purpose attached to it.

For example, Pharaoh dreamed of an impending severe famine. Not only was it going to affect Egypt, but other nations as well, to include Joseph's father homeland. (See Genesis 41:30–31; 42:5.) The favor upon Joseph's life was pivotal for what he was destined to become and accomplish. Joseph's mission was not limited to sparing Egypt from the famine, but he was sent ahead to save his people as well. (See Genesis 45:4–5, 7–8.) Nehemiah is another example of those who receive God's favor to carry out His purpose. Nehemiah was given the support of certain people, including the king, so that he could return to Jerusalem and rebuild a wall that had been destroyed. (See Nehemiah 2:8–9.)

Looking back, many of us can remember times when God's favor was heavy upon our lives and we received blessings we least expected. The favor of God wasn't for us to stockpile or hoard it to ourselves but was an indication that God had something very special and significant for us to do. We must always remember that when we're obedient and our motives are pure, the Lord will bestow His favor upon us to accomplish His will. But we must always remember that the purpose of the favor is for God to always receive glory through our lives!

✦ ✦ ✦

 Further reading, meditation, and study—Nehemiah 2:1–10; Daniel 1:1–21

DOUBLE-MINDEDNESS

But let him ask in faith, with no doubting, for he who doubts is like a wave of the sea driven and tossed by the wind. For let not that man suppose that he will receive anything from the Lord; he is a double-minded man, unstable in all his ways.
—James 1:6–8

Have you ever seen waves of the sea rolling back and forth? I ask this because it gives us a picture of someone who is restless or double-minded. The sea, at times, becomes subject to the forces of the wind, gravity, and high tides. Whenever that happens, the waters will roll back and forth in aggressive way. Likewise, those who are double-minded and unstable are like the sea when the waves are moving back and forth. In the New Testament, James describes a man who begins to ask God for wisdom but soon begins to doubt, not believing that God is able to make good on what he asked of Him. (See James 1:5–8.)

This person is described as a double-minded man unstable in all of his ways. Double-mindedness speaks of people who are always wavering, indecisive, unsure, wishy-washy, doubting, unpredictable, prone to procrastination, and unstable. The Greek word is *"Dipsuchos,"* which literally means "two-souled." Additionally, people who are double-minded have problems making decisions. The moment they make a decision, they struggle to stick with it. As with any strong man, double-mindedness will hinder people from spiritually developing and being all the Father created them to be.

First Corinthians 15:58 says, "Therefore my beloved brethren, be steadfast, immovable, always abounding in the work of the Lord, knowing that your labor is not in vain in the Lord." This scripture speaks volumes. It is the antithesis of those who are unstable. My friend, God's desire for His people is stability. People who are stable are steadfast and immovable. You can count on them not to change their minds every second of the day. You cannot truly love the Lord with all your heart and be double-minded, because it draws your devotion to other things. Every problem, circumstance, or stronghold can be remedied at the cross. Jesus truly came to set the captives free. Please say the prayer below.

Heavenly Father, I come to You in the name of Jesus. I repent of all my sins. I accept what Your Word says about me. I am accepted in the Beloved; I'm a child of God. Lord Jesus, set me free from self-rejection, double-mindedness, depression, despondency, despair, discouragement, hopelessness, unworthiness, rebellion, resentment, unforgiveness, root of bitterness, self-seduction, sabotage, and instability. I close the door to these strongholds. Thank You for setting me completely free. In Jesus's name, I pray. Amen.

DIVINE PROTECTION

For you O Lord are the most High over all the earth;
you are exalted far above all gods, let those who love the
Lord hate evil, for He guards the lives of His faithful
ones and delivers them from the hand of the wicked.
—Psalm 97:9–10

We have to acknowledge there are agents of Satan who are out to hinder, discredit, frustrate, persecute, and ultimately destroy the Lord's work and His anointed. The good news is that God will protect His anointed. When God's anointed are under attack, they're not fighting against flesh and blood. Ephesians 6:12 says, "For our struggle is not against flesh and blood, but against the rulers, against the authorities, against the powers of this dark world and against the spiritual forces of evil in the heavenly realms." God sends a firm warning to those who would allow Satan to use them to attack His anointed ones: "Do not touch My anointed ones; do my prophets no harm" (1 Chronicles 16:22).

This scripture speaks to how God was concerned about the pagan nations' interaction with Israel as they traveled from one place to another. Similarly, the believer in Christ has been grafted in as a result of Christ's atonement. (See John 10:16.) This opens the door for every Christian to receive the many benefits Israel enjoyed— particularly God's protection. David understood what it meant to touch God's anointed, because prior to becoming king, there were times he had Saul right where he wanted him. However, he knew not to touch God's anointed even though Saul walked in rebellion.

This alone gives us comfort and understanding that God protects His anointed at all cost.

When we enter into God's presence, there's safety and protection. Psalm 42:1 says, "… deer pants for the water brook." A deer goes to a brook for several reasons. He goes there firstly because he's thirsty and secondly because when he enters the water, his scent will not be recognized by a pursuing enemy. Through prayer, when we enter God's presence, we receive divine protection. Psalm 31:20 says, "You shall hide them in the secret place of your presence from the plots of man; you shall keep them secretly in a pavilion from the strife of tongues." God is omniscient and omnipresent, and just as He has protected His anointed men and women throughout history, He'll protect us as well.

✧ ✧ ✧

 Further reading, meditation, and study—Psalm 91:1–16; Isaiah 54:17

HELMET OF HOPE

But let us who are of the day be sober, putting on the
breastplate of faith and love and as a helmet the hope
of salvation. For God did appoint us to wrath, but to
attain salvation through our Lord Jesus Christ.
—1 Thessalonian 5:8–9

The mind is the most vulnerable area Satan often attacks. In the most
predatory way, he tries to infiltrate it with negative thoughts. If he
succeeds, we become ineffective in our walks with Christ and our
war against him. Peter warns us against this type of demonic strategy.
1 Peter 5:8 says, "Be sober, be vigilant; because your adversary the
devil walks about like a roaring lion seeking whom he may devour."
Soldiers in combat will never fight without their helmets because
they know they'll sustain head injuries if they do so. Similarly, if
we're wounded spiritually in our minds, we'll become ineffective in
all areas of our spiritual walks.

What is our defensive barrier to keeping the enemy from attacking
our minds? Paul gives us the answer: "Therefore take up the whole
armor of God that you may be able to withstand in the evil day
and having done all to stand ... and take the helmet of salvation"
(Ephesians 6:12, 17). The helmet of salvation is part of the spiritual
equipment that keeps the enemy from attacking and wounding our
minds. When Paul admonishes us to put on the helmet, this clearly
places the responsibility on us. First Thessalonians 5:8 says, "But let
us who are of the day be sober, putting on the breastplate of faith and
love and as a helmet the hope of salvation."

The helmet of salvation is also the hope of salvation. This sheds light on how hope protects our minds. Hope is a quiet, steady expectation of good based on the promises of God's Word. Faith is the foundation and reality in which hope is built. Once we have faith, we then have valid hope. (See Romans 15:4.) Hope is a continuing optimism: a mind that always chooses to see the best and will not give way to depression, doubt, and self-pity. When we allow the Holy Spirit to have access and authority over our minds, combined with the helmet of hope, we'll have victory over every obstacle and every enemy.

✧ ✧ ✧

 Further reading, meditation, and study—Romans 15:1–6; 1 Thessalonians 5:1–11

EGYPT OR PROMISED LAND

In [this] freedom Christ has made us free [and completely liberated us] stand fast then, and do not be hampered and held ensnared and submit again to a yoke of slavery [which you have once put off].
—Galatians 5:1 (AMP)

In the Old Testament, Ruth and Orpah had to make a decision concerning their destinies to either go back to a sort of Egypt or choose to move forward to a kind of Promised Land. Their story begins with both of them losing their husbands and father-in-law while in Moab (symbolic of Egypt). During the course of time, their mother-in-law Naomi decides it is time to return to Bethlehem (symbolic of the Promised Land) since she has heard that God visited her people and ended the famine. As a result of Naomi's decision, Ruth and Orpah are put in a difficult position. I'm sure questions surfaced in their minds: "Should I remain in Moab?" or "What will become of me? Is there a future for me in Bethlehem?"

Ruth decided to go back with her mother-in-law, but Orpah decided to stay in her homeland of Moab. (See Ruth 1:14–16.) No way would Ruth have known that her response, "Your God, my God," would be pivotal and have great significance in the future. That confession alone straightforwardly rejected the false gods in Moab and opened the door for many blessings upon her life. The Moabites didn't worship the God of the Israelites; instead they served multiple false gods. (See Ruth 1:15.) Ruth and Orpah are symbolic of how believers can either move forward or return to dead things—how they can choose freedom or revert back to bondage.

Sadly, many believers in Christ find it safe to go back to what

283

they are accustomed to or familiar with. We should never, under any circumstance, return to dead things. (See Luke 9:57–62.) When Lot and his family were fleeing to safety, Lot's wife looked back and was turned into a pillar of salt. There will always be consequences for looking back or turning back. As believers in Christ, we should always have a willingness to move forward. People who are determined to go backward will either miss their season of opportunity or, worse, fall from grace.

📖   Further reading, meditation, and study—Ruth 1:1–22; Luke 9:57–62

EFFECTIVE COMMUNICATOR

You are fairer than the sons of men; grace is poured
upon Your lips; therefore, God has blessed You
forever …You have righteousness and hate wickedness;
therefore, God, Your God, has anointed You, with
the oil of gladness more than Your companions.
—Psalm 45:1, 7

Words truly have enormous power, and our Lord Jesus knows how significant they are. One of the characteristics I love and admire about Jesus during His time on Earth is His ability to communicate effectively. He was a master at using the right words and knowing how to communicate with people. While on Earth, His life was one of truth, holiness, love, compassion, transparency, honesty, candidness, and bluntness. When He spoke, the people around Him were amazed; even His enemies had to take notice. Matthew 7:28–29 says, "And so it was, when Jesus had ended these sayings, that the people were astonished at His teaching, for He taught them as one having authority, and not as the scribes."

Jesus knew the importance of speaking with love and humility, but He also knew how to speak with boldness and authority. What set Him apart from His peers was a lifestyle that backed what He said and taught. When it came to living a life of holiness and truthfulness, the Pharisees and religious leaders (His enemies) were a total contradiction in light of how Christ lived. Jesus, at various times, was bold in how He spoke and responded to people, but He was also very gracious with His words. (See Luke 4:16–22.) Jesus never used words to condemn anyone. He knew how to bring restoration and deliverance to those who were guilty.[16]

When Christ spoke, His words were filled with Spirit and life. (See John 6:63.) In the midst of darkness and uncertainty, Jesus's mercy and gracious words illuminated the atmosphere. In the perilous times in which we now live, His words still illuminate people's lives. We can learn a lot from Him, because words that are ministered without the Holy Spirit are just mere words, but words empowered and endorsed by the Holy Spirit will transform lives. It's not enough just to speak the truth; it has to be done in a gracious manner. The gracious words that poured out of Christ's mouth attracted people from all walks of life, and His words of grace still attract and save those who are lost today.

✧ ✧ ✧

 Further reading, meditation, and study—Psalm 45:1–7; Luke 4:16–22

GOOD, ACCEPTABLE, AND PERFECT

*And do not be conformed to this world, but be transformed
by the renewing of your mind, that you may prove what
is that good and acceptable and perfect will of God.*
—Romans 12:2

While on earth, Jesus was not out to satisfy His human and earthly desires but His heavenly Father's will and purpose. John 6:38 says, "For I have come down from heaven not to do my will but to do the will of Him who sent Me." God wants us to deny ourselves and to take up our crosses. The moment we make that decision, His will become ours. A preacher once said, "Your cross is the place where your will and God's will cross each other." Everyone who has surrendered his or her life to Christ has come to this place in his or her walk. He or she has made a bold declaration and resolution that he or she will choose God's will over his or her own.

The will of God is always best, but many are afraid of embracing it for their lives. (See Romans 12:2.) One important thing every Christian will have to do is come to the end of himself or herself. Consider what Jesus told His disciples: "I tell you the truth unless a kernel of wheat falls to the ground and dies, it remains only a single seed, but if it dies it produces many seeds" (John 12:24). Denying and dying to oneself is one of the primary keys to being in the center of God's will. Following are a few essential facts concerning the will of God.

First, the will of God will always line up with the Bible. (See Psalm 119:105.) Second, God's specific will for our lives can be confirmed over time through prophesy and peace ruling in our hearts. (See Colossians 3:15.) Third, God's Word, combined with true peace, will settle the clash between our wills and God's will. Finally, by embracing God's will, we bestow honor and glory upon Him. Remember that we were created to bring Him glory. (See 1 Corinthians 10:31; Revelation 4:11.) Carrying out the will comes with many inconveniences and personal sacrifices, but we'll discover that it's good, acceptable, and perfect.

✧✧✧

It's only when we've totally yielded and surrendered
to the Holy Spirit that we'll be able to live according
to and carry out God's will for our lives.

 Further reading, meditation, and study—John 6:34–40; Romans 12:1–2

GOD'S INSTRUMENTS

Brothers think of what you were when you were called. Not many
of you were wise by human standards; not many were influential;
not many were of noble birth. But God chose the foolish things
of the world to shame the wise; God chose the weak things of
the world to shame the strong. He chose the lowly things of this
world and the despised things and the things that are not, to
nullify the things that are so that no one may boast before him.
—1 Corinthians 1:26–29 (NIV)

Prior to surrendering to Christ, we were dead in trespasses and sins,
walking according to the course of this world, sons of disobedience
and, by nature, children of wrath. Not many of us were wise by
human standards and influential according to society. Nonetheless,
God saved us through His Son, Jesus, and set us apart by the Holy
Spirit for His divine purpose. He reached down in the trash pile of
life and pulled us out. And what's even more astonishing is that "we
have this treasure in earthen vessels, that the excellence of the power
may be of God and not of us" (2 Corinthians 4:1).

Consider David's appointment to kingship. First Samuel 16:6–7
says, "Samuel saw Eliab and thought, surely the Lord's anointed stands
here before the Lord. But the Lord said to Samuel, do not consider
his appearance or his height, for I have rejected him. The Lord
does not look at the things man looks at. Man looks at the outward
appearance, but the Lord looks at the heart." God's qualifications are
very distinct from how human wisdom chooses a man. Samuel used
logic and human wisdom as he looked for a king among Jesse's sons.

This is exactly how human wisdom works. It looks at how tall, how smart, how rich, and how popular one is.

When Jesus called His disciples, they were comprised of fishermen, tax collectors, and some occupations unknown. Just think; the apostle Paul had a ruthless background history. Nonetheless, after he was converted he was commissioned to carry out God's purpose in spite of his background. He also wrote more epistles than any of his contemporaries, and signs and wonders followed his ministry. Paul's résumé should encourage us by letting us know God chooses ordinary people to do extraordinary things in His kingdom.

📖 Further reading, meditation, and study—Romans 12:1–2; 1 Corinthians 1:20–31

EFFECTS OF GOD'S WORD

All Scripture is given by inspiration of God, and is profitable for doctrine, for reproof, for correction, for instruction in righteousness, that the man of God may be complete, thoroughly equipped for every good work.
—2 Timothy 3:16–17

Kingdom work is very important and should never be neglected or taken lightly. The Word of God is also crucial to our walk with God and overcoming circumstances. There are at least nine effects of the Word. First, we obtain faith because most people struggle to overcome their circumstances. Romans 10:17 says, "So then faith comes by hearing, and hearing by the Word of God." Second, the Word of God plays an important role in salvation. James 1:18 says, "Of His own will He brought us forth by the word of truth [Bible], that we might be a kind of first fruits of His creatures." Third, we receive spiritual nourishment. Every day, we need two types of nourishment: physical and spiritual food. Jesus said, "Man shall not live by bread alone, but by every word that proceeds from the mouth of God" (Matthew 4:4). Fourth, we receive spiritual illumination. When we're faced with circumstances, we need understanding and guidance. Psalm 119:130 says, "The entrance of Your words give light; it gives understanding to the simple." Fifth, we receive physical healing. Psalm 107:20 says, "He sent His Word and healed them, and delivered them from their destructions." The three great acts of God's mercy and grace are salvation from sin, healing from sickness, and deliverance from demonic power. All are accomplished through His Word. Sixth, we receive victory over sin. Psalm 119:9, 11 says,

"How can a young man cleanse his way? By taking heed according to Your word …Your word I have hidden in my heart, that I might not sin against you." Counseling has its place, but what turns people from sin is reading God's Word and applying it in their lives. Finally, the Word of God is our spiritual mirror. James 1:25 says, "But the man who looks intently into the perfect law that gives freedom, and continues to do this, not forgetting what he has heard, but doing it he will be blessed in what he does." Whenever we're faced with things beyond our control, we can open the Bible and receive instruction in righteousness and everything that pertains to life and godliness.

✧✧✧

 Further reading, meditation, and study—2 Timothy 3:14–17; James 1:21–25

THE ADMINISTRATOR

I have much more to say to you, more than you can now bear,
but when He the Spirit of truth comes, He will guide you into
all truth. He will not speak on His own; He will speak only what
He hears, and He will tell you what is yet to come. He will bring
glory to Me by taking what is Mine and making it known to
you. All that belongs to the Father is Mine that is why I said the
Spirit will take from what is Mine and make it known to you.
—John 16:12–15

When my grandparents passed away in the midseventies, they left my
aunt as the administrator. After she passed, another relative assumed
the role, and so on. In subsequent years, the administrator was to
run, manage, direct, and govern the estate. The Holy Spirit is the
Administrator of the assets and wealth of the Godhead. He is the one
that makes it available to us.

Let's look at a few riches of heaven the Father made available
through the Holy Spirit. He comforts us. There are multitudes of sad
people in society. What they need is the comfort of the Holy Spirit.
(See John 14:16.) He teaches and brings things to our remembrance.
Have you ever studied the Bible and received wonderful insights
into a particular scripture? The Holy Spirit is imparting revelation
and bringing things to your remembrance. (See John14:26.) He
convicts us of sin. The Holy Spirit will not allow us to ignore sin.
He'll bring conviction. (See John 16:7–8.) He guides us into all truth.
The reason He's able to guide us is because He doesn't speak on His
own authority. (See John 16:13.) He glorifies Jesus. The Holy Spirit
will ensure the Father is glorified when we operate in the kingdom.

(See John 16:14.) He's the source of power. In order to be effective witnesses and be witnesses for Christ, we need His enablement and power. (See Acts1:8.)

Finally, He helps us while we pray. There are moments when we don't know how to pray or what to pray about. There's good news: the Holy Spirit will help us. (See Romans 8:26.) The Holy Spirit is our spiritual guide and administrator of the riches of God's kingdom. He is the one that imparts spiritual blessings to us from the throne of God. There's no reason for God's children to forfeit spiritual things that have been given as a result of the atoning work of Christ. Jesus has paved the way and paid a tremendous price.

✧✧✧

 Further reading, meditation, and study—John 16:5–15; 2 Corinthians 1:20–22

NOT A LICENSE

What shall we say then, shall we continue in sin that grace
may abound? Certainly not! How shall we who died to
sin live any longer in it ...What then? Shall we sin because
we are not under law but under grace? Certainly not!
—Romans 6:1–2, 15

Are you aware there are multitudes of Christians who minimize the sinfulness of sin? They believe that how they live has very little to do with their faith. The truth is that what a person truly believes will show up in how he or she lives. Christians who have genuine faith will demonstrate it by their deep respect and reverence for God. Sadly, there are some who believe that they have a license to sin and that God will give them a pass. However, this is not what the Bible teaches. Romans 6:1–2 says, "What shall we say then, shall we continue in sin that grace may abound? Certainly not! How shall we who died to sin live any longer in it."

Furthermore, some people's attitude toward grace and sin goes something like this: "If God loves to forgive, then why not sin more?" To commit premeditated and habitual sin and assume God will graciously forgive is really tempting Him. The availability of God's grace must not become an excuse for careless and sinful living. The grace of God is a widely misunderstood subject especially for people who live habitual lives of sin. The truth about grace is that it's God's unmerited favor toward the undeserving but never a means to compromise or sin.

There's a high level of responsibility that comes with hearing and knowing the truth. Once we gain spiritual knowledge about something, we're held responsible. This is similar to what Jesus says: "To whom much is given much is required" (Luke 12:48). Jesus made this very clear to an impotent man whom he had healed. He gave the man enough grace for his present condition but told him, "Sin no more, lest a worse thing come unto thee" (John 5:14). We must always bear in mind that just because God's grace and mercy are accessible and available in the person of Christ Jesus doesn't mean it's a license to sin.

✧✧✧

 Further reading, meditation, and study—John 5:1–14; Romans 6:1–15

COME TO JESUS

Come to Me, all you who labor and are heavy laden, and I
will give you rest. Take My yoke upon you and learn from
Me, for I am gentle and lowly in heart, and you will find rest
for your souls. For My yoke is easy and My burden is light.
—Matthew 11:28–30

I have heard the above scripture ministered in a variety of ways,
all of them good. But some have placed a limit on who Jesus was
referring to when He said, "Come to Me." They tend to think He's
referring only to sinners, but a closer look reveals that He is speaking
to a diverse class of people in various scenarios. It's a clarion call
for everyone who needs Him. Although we must come to Jesus for
salvation, we should come to Him for everything we encounter in
this life. (See 1 Peter 5:7.) During Jesus's time on earth, there were
multitudes of people who came to Him, but unlike the religious sect
that rejected Him, many didn't receive His invitation in vain.

The religious people often rejected Him because of His message,
but those who needed help saw Him as their solution. Christ's
invitation is for everyone who is bound and overburdened. For
instance, carnal and worldly Christians burden themselves with cares
of life (wealth, pleasure, and prestige). Unbelievers and sinners are
laden with sinful lifestyles contrary to the Bible, Christians who
operate in legalism are overburdened by attempting to establish their
own righteousness apart from Christ's righteousness, Christians who
are overburdened with an array of things God hasn't commissioned
them to do are weighted down, and so on.

Christ says to these classes of people and more, "Come to Me.

Cease from fruitless and demanding spiritual labor. Cease from a life of sin and pleasure. Cease trying to establish your own righteousness. Give Me the heavy load and yoke you placed upon yourself, and take My yoke and learn from Me, and I'll give you rest for your souls." When Jesus says we are to come to Him, He's implying that serving Him is not hard and demanding. In fact, His burden is light. He came to set captives free from every form of bondage known to man. Submitting and embracing His message of grace and truth contradicts many things we sometimes impose upon ourselves.

✦ ✦ ✦

 Further reading, meditation, and study—Matthew 11:28–30; Hebrews 12:1–3

SYROPHOENICIAN WOMEN

Then Jesus answered and said to her, O woman,
great is your faith! Let it be to you as you desire. And
her daughter was healed from that very hour.
—Matthew 15:21–28

Many people can relate to the story of the Syrophoenician woman and her daughter. Her faith was tremendously tested. Observe the anguish and desperation in her voice: "She cried out to Him, saying have mercy on me, O Lord, Son of David!" (v. 22). But notice that Jesus answered her not a word and His disciples urged Him to send her away (v. 23). Just think; not only was she confronted with the suffering of her daughter, but what looked like silence and rejection were added to her situation.

Although it may seem the Lord isn't responding, He has heard our prayers since the moment we began to pray. The Lord told Daniel, "Do not fear, for from the first day that you set your heart to understand, and to humble yourself before your God, your words were heard" (Daniel 10:12). Similar to what the angel told Daniel, we must believe that God has heard our prayers from the moment we began to pray. The Lord "hears the prayers of the righteous" and "the effective, fervent prayer of a righteous man avails much" (Proverbs 15:29; James 5:16).

It's easy to give up and throw in the towel when it seems like your breakthrough is not on the horizon, but we must be very persistent in our prayers to God. This is similar to the widow who kept going before an unjust judge who didn't fear God or regard man but eventually granted her request. There must be a resolve to see a change in our circumstances as well. Luke 18:1 says, "Then He [Jesus] spoke a parable to them, that men always ought to pray and not lose heart." God may not always come when we expect Him, but He's always on time.

✧✧✧

 Further reading, meditation, and study—Matthew 15:21–28; Luke 18:1–8

✧ ✧ ✧

Remember the word to Your servant, upon which You have
caused me to hope. This is my comfort in my affliction,
for Your word has given me life ... Forever, O Lord Your
word is settled in heaven ... Your word is a lamp to my feet
and a light to my path ... You are my hiding place and my
shield; I hope in Your word ... Consider my affliction and
deliver me, for I do not forget Your law. Plead my cause
and redeem me; revive me according to Your word.

—Psalm 119:48–50, 89, 105, 114, 153–154

SECTION 2

✧✧✧

PROCLAMATIONS AND CONFESSIONS

Encouraging Scriptures to Proclaim and Confess
When Faced with Life's Circumstances

Proclaiming and Confessing the Word of God

For as the rain comes down, and the snow from heaven, and do
not return there but water the earth, and make it bring forth
and bud. That it may give seed to the sower and bread to the
eater. So shall My word be that goes forth from My mouth;
it shall not return to Me void, but it shall accomplish what I
please, and it shall prosper in the thing for which I sent it.
—Isaiah 55:10–11

There's enormous power released through proclaiming and
confessing the Word of God. These are two powerful resources that
are often neglected. Whatever the magnitude of our personal needs
or circumstances, it's through prayer, proclamation, and confession
that they can be solved. Some Christians have either forgotten or
haven't realized we can speak the Word to our mountains. (See
Matthew 17:20.) Proclaiming and confessing God's Word calls forth
God's intervention and His supernatural and creative power. Psalm
119:89 says, "Forever, O Lord, Your word is settled in heaven." To
know we have the privilege of speaking God's eternal Word over
life's circumstances is absolutely a blessing.

Proclaiming and confessing the Scriptures is an extremely
important role of every Christian. First we must allow the Word to
be planted and rooted within our hearts. David wrote, "Your word
I have hidden in my heart …" (Psalm 119:11). Jesus said "… Man
shall not live by bread alone, but every word that proceeds from
the mouth of God" (Matthew 4:4). Christians who have the Word
planted in their hearts are not afraid to proclaim it with boldness

and confidence through their mouths. Remember that Jesus said, "For out of the abundance of the heart the mouth speaks" (Matthew 12:34). The moment God's Word is released out of our mouths, He will faithfully watch over it to perform it. (See Jeremiah 1:12.)

Additionally, life and death are in the power of the tongue. (See Proverbs 18:21.) The Word we speak is spirit and life. (See John 6:63.) This alone shows that proclaiming God's Word releases supernatural power for breakthroughs in our lives and the lives of others. The Bible is essentially God's thoughts; we're calling forth His mind into a situation the moment we pray, confess, and proclaim His Word. For example, Jeremiah 29:11 says, "For I know the thoughts that I think toward you, says the Lord, thoughts of peace and not of evil, to give you a future and a hope." Just think; this is God's thoughts toward His people, and when we confess and proclaim His Word, we receive by faith what He has declared about us.

The word "proclaim" is a strong word. It comes from a Latin word that means "shout forth." It's a word in the New Testament that means "to confess." "Confess" means "to say the same as." As believers in Christ, we're saying with our mouths what God has already declared and decreed in His Word. To say it another way, we allow our mouths and tongues to come into agreement with the Word of God. The moment we make that decision, we have the full backing of the Father, Son, and the Holy Spirit. Remember: Jesus is the "High Priest of our confession" (Hebrews 3:1). When we confess and proclaim what the Bible has promised and written about us as believers, we then have Jesus as a High Priest releasing His power, authority, and blessings upon us and our circumstances.

James 5:16 says, "The effective, fervent prayer of a righteous man avails much." It's very important and effective to proclaim God's Word in prayer. Praying in faith and proclaiming the Word can move mountains. Jesus said there's nothing impossible to those who believe. Whatever we ask in prayer by faith, confessing, proclaiming, and believing, we will receive. Matthew 21:21–22 says, "So Jesus answered and said to them, assuredly, I say to you if you have faith and do not doubt, you will not only do what was done to this fig tree, but also if you say to this mountain, be removed and be cast into the sea, it will be done. And whatever things you ask in prayer, believing you will receive."

You may be asking by now what is meant by "proclaim" or "proclamation." Proclaiming is essentially the activity of a herald. In medieval times, a herald was a person with authority from a king or nobleman. We can also add modern-day ambassadors as examples as well. A herald would enter a public place and make a proclamation of the desires and will of the one who sent him. He would shout out something to the effect of "Oyez, Oyez!" and proceed with the proclamation. When the people heard it, they knew it was the voice of authority and heeded what he said. Likewise, when we proclaim God's Word, we're speaking with authority and boldness because we know we're declaring God's desire and will.

A proclamation is a confession that's assertive. "Proclamation" is a word that speaks of spiritual warfare. The reason I say this is because it's releases the authority of God's Word into a circumstance or situation. Proclamation releases God's Word into your personal life, the lives of your family members, the life of your church or ministry, and so on. There are multitudes of hurting people who are enduring hard and unspeakable circumstances. What they often need is someone to pray, proclaim, or speak the Word with faith to their mountains. Jesus said, "If you have faith as a mustard seed, you will say to this mountain, move from here to there and it will move and nothing will be impossible for you" (Matthew 17:20).

Christians who read and study the Bible have knowledge of God's divine will. When we know something is God's will, we can proclaim it and expect positive results. This is stated for us in 1 John 5:14–15: "And this is the confidence (the assurance, the privilege of boldness) which we have in Him; [we are sure] that if we ask anything (make any request) according to His will (in agreement with His own plan); He listens to and hears us. And if (since) we [positively] know that He listen to us in whatever we ask, we also know [with settled and absolute knowledge] that we have [granted us as our present possessions] the requests made of Him."

There's protection through proclamation and confessing the Word of God. We can be model citizens and keep to ourselves, but there will always be those who don't like us, speak against us, or even pray against us for whatever reason. If that should happen, we must proclaim and confess the Word of God over our lives and our loved ones. The remedy for someone speaking negative words over us is laid out in Isaiah 54:17: "No weapon that is formed against us shall prosper, and every tongue that rises against us in judgment we do condemn. This is our heritage as servants of the Lord, and our righteousness is from You [God], O Lord of Hosts."

Proclaiming and confessing God's righteousness and not our own will confuses the devil and his assaults against us. One reason for this is that the devil and his servants have refused God's righteousness, and that alone places them in a fight they cannot win. Additionally, proclamation condemns the devil's verbal assaults against us. There's power in the tongue, and we must immediately cast down any unwholesome words sent against us. (See Proverbs 18:21; 2 Corinthians 10:5.) God has given us power over the enemy. (See Luke 10:19.) Whenever we come under attack, we must immediately proclaim and confess the Word of God.

For instance, Jesus was led up by the Spirit into the wilderness to be tempted by the devil. (See Matthew 4:1.) The Lord's encounter with the devil gives us the rules of engagement. Jesus came under persistent verbal temptations by the devil, but He proclaimed the Word to him every time. Three consecutive times, Jesus answered and said "It is written, man shall not live by bread alone, but by every word that proceeds from the mouth of God ... It is written again, you shall not tempt the Lord, your God ... Away with you, Satan! For it is written, you shall worship the Lord your God, and Him only you shall serve" (vv. 4–10).

It's imperative that you "study to show thyself approved unto God, a workman that needeth not to be ashamed, rightly dividing the word of truth" (2 Timothy 2:15 KJV). This admonition is not only for righteous living, times of need, or service in the kingdom; it is an admonition to recall the Word in times of attacks from the enemy. A lack of knowledge concerning the Word of God leaves us with no defensive measures and an empty confession. The enemy knows there's power when we confess and proclaim the Word of God. The devil is no match or threat to our Lord and Savior, Jesus. He is the Word made flesh, and He knows how to execute it.

Prayer encompasses more than just thanksgiving, worship, and petitions. It involves proclaiming, confessing, and speaking the Word of God while we pray. I stated earlier that Jesus said we should speak to our mountains. When we speak and proclaim the Word of God, it gets the enemy's attention and puts him on the run. The devil trembles at God's Word, not our rhetoric, reasoning, and logic. Jeremiah 23:29 says, "'Is not My word like a fire?' says the Lord, and like a hammer that breaks the rock in pieces." We can overcome every attack and scheme by the devil through the power of proclaiming and confessing God's Word.

The devil is a liar and schemer. (See John 8:44.) A scheme is a plan, design, and course of action. Natural and spiritual warfare involves tactics and strategies. The greatest wars are won through generals and commanders who are great tacticians and strategists. Victories are often won as a result of wise and strong strategies. When the Bible says we're not ignorant of Satan's devices, it means we must never allow the enemy to strategize against us. Revelation 12:11 says, "And they overcame him by the blood of the Lamb and by the word of their testimony, and they did not love their lives to death."

The phrase "the word of their testimony" means we are to testify to what the blood of Christ has done for us. We must make it personal. Remember: we're testifying to Satan through proclaiming and confessing the Word of God. Another way of saying it is that we're letting him know what the Word of God has promised through the atonement of Christ. For example, we testify that according to Ephesians 1:7, "In Him [Jesus] we have redemption through His blood, the forgiveness of sins according to the riches of His grace." We don't stop there. We testify according to Romans 5:9: "Much more then, having now been justified by His blood, we shall be saved from wrath through Him [Jesus]."

To be justified means to be made righteous. At the cross, there was a divine exchange made on our behalf. We were made righteous with Christ's righteousness. The moment we fully embrace this, the devil cannot continue to accuse us before God. In other words, Satan's main weapon has been taken away from him. The devil is persistent and relentless, accusing us before God. He has to hear from our mouths that we have been justified by the blood of Jesus and have been made righteous as if we have never sinned. This strips him of his argument in the courts of heaven and throws out his case against us. This is why it's so important to "Hold fast the confession of our hope without wavering, for He [Christ] who promised is faithful" (Hebrews 10:23).

In Paul's list of spiritual armor in Ephesians 6:14–17, we learn there are five items in that armor that are primarily for defending against the enemy. The defensive list includes truth, the breastplate of righteousness, preparation of the gospel of peace, the shield of faith, and the helmet of salvation. These all protect us from vicious attacks from the kingdom of darkness. But there's only one weapon of offense, or weapon of attack, and that is the sword of the Spirit, which is the Word of God. (See also Hebrews 4:12.)

Most preachers stress the importance of defending oneself against the enemy, but rarely do you hear messages that focus on attacking the devil. If we want to put Satan and his demonic kingdom on the run, stop him from harassing us and our families, evict him from our homes, places of business, and ministries, the weapon we must use is the sword of Spirit. "Word of God" is the primary translation of the word "*rhema*," which denotes a word that is spoken. When we proclaim and confess the Word of God boldly and with confidence, it becomes a sharp two-edged sword in our mouths.

Earlier we learned the meaning of "proclamation." Let's look briefly at the word "confession." "Confession" means "to say the same as." As believers in Christ, to us it means we're saying with our mouths what God has already declared and decreed in His Word. David wrote, "Let the words of my mouth and the meditation of my heart be acceptable in Your sight, O Lord, my strength and my

Redeemer" (Psalm 19:14). David allowed his mouth to agree and line up with the Father. He understood that it would please Him. The moment we allow our mouths to come in agreement with what the Word declares, we have the full assurance and backing of the Father, Son, and Holy Spirit.

Whenever we confess and proclaim what the Bible has promised and written about, we have Jesus as a High Priest releasing His power, authority, and blessings upon us and our circumstances. (See Hebrews 3:1.) What's more, we have His blessings upon what He has already declared. But there are negative consequences when we choose to reject His Word and walk in unbelief. In the book of Numbers, there's a story that really brings home this point. It's about Moses sending out twelve men to spy out the land of Canaan. Keep in mind that God had already promised He would give them land flowing with milk and honey.

The spies set out on their journey and returned after forty days. Interestingly enough, upon return they initially gave a positive report of how the land did, in fact, flow with milk and honey. They even brought back pomegranates, figs, and large clusters of grapes. However, things began to turn for the worse when they decided to give a negative report of the land, despite what God had spoken. Numbers 13:28 says, "Nevertheless the people who dwell in the land are strong; the cities are fortified and very large; moreover, we saw the descendants of Anak there." The report they shared didn't line up with what God initially told them. Sadly, they focused more on what they had seen rather than what God had spoken.

According to verse 30, "Caleb quieted the people before Moses and said, let us go up at once and take possession, for we are well able to overcome it." At this point, the Israelites had an opportunity to reverse their confession of doubt and unbelief, but they double down on what they previously said. Verse 31 says, "But the men who had gone up with him said, we are not able to go up against the people, for they are stronger than we and they gave the children of Israel a bad report of the land ..." Caleb's confession is important for us to grasp. When you believe what God has declared, you'll speak the same things that God has spoken.

We should avoid negative-speaking people—especially those who try to change our confessions. Similar to Jesus rebuking Peter, we might have to rebuke those who stand in the way of God's purposes. Similarly, the ten spies' negative confession caused the people to doubt God's promises. Numbers 14:1 says, "So all the congregation lifted up their voices and cried, and the people wept that night. And all the children of Israel complained against Moses and Aaron, and the whole congregation said to them, if only we had died in the land of Egypt! If only we had died in this wilderness. Why has the Lord brought us to this land to fall by the sword, that our wives and children should become victims? Would it not be better for us to return to Egypt?"

It's important to see that the receipt of that negative report caused complaining and murmuring among the people. But further down, in Numbers 24, my eyes were drawn to verse 24: "But My servant Caleb, because he has a different spirit in him and has followed Me fully, I will bring into the land where he went, and his descendants shall inherit it." Here we read that God makes a reference to Caleb's spirit. This is not the same spirit within the Israelites, but a different spirit. It is my belief that when people doubt God and speak negatively, they have spirits of unbelief.

We must always be careful whom we listen to and align ourselves with. Just as bad company corrupts good morals, people who have spirits of unbelief will pollute our thinking and our responses to God's instructions and promises. Because of the Israelites' negative confessions, God's anger was kindled against them. As a result, everyone twenty years old and above did not enter the Promised Land, with the exception of Caleb and Joshua. (See Numbers 14:30.) We can learn quite a lot from their experiences; we must always come into agreement with the Word of God and refuse to walk in doubt and unbelief. In the New Testament, we see another example of someone given a Word from God, but this time it was embraced wholeheartedly. Mary, prior to giving birth to Jesus, came into agreement with what the Lord spoke concerning her.

> And the angel answered and said to her, the Holy Spirit will come upon you, and the power of the Highest will overshadow you; therefore, also that Holy One who is to be born will be called the Son of God. Now indeed, Elizabeth your relative has also conceived a son in her old age; and this is now the sixth month for her who was called barren. For with God nothing will be impossible. Then Mary said, behold the maidservant of the Lord! Let it be to me according to your word, and the angel departed from her. (Luke 1:35–38)

When Mary said, "Let it be to me according to your word," (v. 38), Her response is the true definition of what is meant by "confession." Mary didn't stagger in unbelief but came into agreement with what God had said concerning her. Similarly, when we read the Bible, hear a message, or receive a true prophetic word, we should say, "Let it be to me according to His Word." However, before we can claim God's promises in His Word, we must know what they are. So I would like to share different categories of major promises from God. But before I do, I believe it's important to show why the Word of God and the Scriptures are so important. "Jesus answered them, is it not written in your law, I said you are gods. If He called them gods, to whom the Word of God came (and the Scripture cannot be broken), do you say of Him whom the Father sanctified and sent into the world, you are blaspheming, because I said, I am the Son of God?" (John 10:34–36).

Here Jesus is speaking to a group of Jews and defending the claim that He is the Son of God, a right He had previously made and which they had contested. In response, Jesus brings to light two important titles that have been used by all Christians to designate the Bible as the Word of God and the Scripture. So that we can appreciate God's promises, let's look briefly at these two titles, which tell us a lot about the nature of the Bible. By calling the Bible "the Word of God" when speaking to the Jews, Jesus indicated that the truths revealed in it originate not with humans, but with God. Second Peter 1:20 says, "Knowing this first, that no prophecy of Scripture is of any private interpretation, for prophecy never came by the will of man, by holy men of God spoke as they were moved by the Holy Spirit."

Although many men wrote the Bible and were used in a variety of ways to communicate it to the world, they were instruments and channels. Every time we hear someone preach or teach God's Word, the message did not originate with him or her. The person is communicating what God spoke in His Word. It's important to note that God's Word must be received as though God is speaking directly to you. First Thessalonians 1:13 (AMP) says, "And we also [especially] thank God continually by this that which you receive the message of God [which you heard] from us, you welcome it not as the word of [mere] men, but as it truly is, the word of God, which is effectually at work in you who believe [exercising its superhuman power in those who adhere to and trust in rely on it]."

The second title Jesus used is "the Scripture" (John 10:35). The Scripture consists of divine quotes and sections of the Bible. The phrase "the Scripture" literally means "that which is written." Notice that when Jesus used the phrase "the Scripture," He added something that negates and counteracts any false narrative against the Bible. He said, "The Scripture cannot be broken" (v. 35). In other words, the Bible is the supreme and divine authority of God and cannot be broken. Psalm 119:89 says, "Forever, O Lord, Your word is settled in heaven." Because the Scriptures cannot be broken and they're settled in heaven, we have the assurance of all the promises of God.

Second Timothy 3:16–17 says, "All Scripture is given by inspiration is given by inspiration of God, and is profitable for doctrine, for reproof, for correction, for instruction in righteousness, that the man of God may be complete, thoroughly equipped for every good work." The word "inspiration" means "inbreathed of God and directly associated with the word 'Spirit.'" In other words, God's Spirit or the Holy Spirit was the invisible influence who controlled and directed the men who wrote the books of the Bible. (See 2 Peter 1:20.) One other thing I should mention is that the Bible is the product of eternity. Between the pages, it contains the eternal mind and counsel of God created before the foundation of the world. (See Psalm 119:89.)

Finally, the Word of God and the Scriptures are truth. Psalm 119:160 says, "The entirety of Your word is truth, and every one of Your righteous judgments endures forever." This is so important for us to grasp. God is a God who cannot speak a lie, and because of that His Word can always be trusted. (See Hebrews 6:18.) Since the Scriptures are completely God's words, and because He does not speak falsely, we can conclude that there's no untruthfulness or error in any parts of Bible. Proverbs 30:5 says, "Every word of God is pure; He is a shield to those who put their trust in Him."

Thus far we have learned some important things concerning the Word of God and the Scriptures. Since the entirety of the Bible is truth, we should embrace what it says about us as believers in Christ. On the following page, I have made a list of various categories of scriptures relating to God's promises from the Bible. Proclaim and confess them over your circumstances. It would be a great idea also to speak them daily over your personal life, family, friends, coworkers, business, and ministry. They are intended to help build your confidence and faith to believe. Remember: faith comes by hearing, and hearing by the Word of God. (See Romans 10:17.)

GOD'S PROMISES FOR HEALTH AND HEALING

I am the Lord that heals you.
—Exodus 15:26

No evil shall befall you, nor shall any plague
Come near your dwelling.
—Psalm 91:10

Bless the Lord, O my soul, and forget not all His benefits....
Who Heals all your diseases, Who redeems
your life from destruction.
—Psalm 103:2–4

He saved them out of their distresses, He sent His word
And healed them, and delivered them.
—Psalm 107:19–20

He was wounded for our transgressions, He was bruised for our
Iniquities ... and by His stripes we are healed.
—Isaiah 53:5

Behold, and I will bring it health and healing; I will heal them
and reveal to them the abundance of peace and truth.
—Jeremiah 33:6

To you who fear My name, the Sun of Righteousness
Shall arise with healing in His wings.
—Malachi 4:2

That it might be fulfilled which was spoken
by Isaiah the prophet saying,
He Himself took our infirmities and bore our sicknesses.
—Matthew 8:17

Who Himself bore our sins in His own body
on the tree, that we, having died
to sins, might live for righteousness by
whose stripes you were healed.
—1 Peter 2:24

God's Promises for Hope and Assurance

Oh, love the Lord, all you His Saints! For
the Lord preserves the faithful
and repays the proud person. Be of good courage, and He shall
strengthen your heart, all you who hope in the Lord.
—Psalm 31:23–24

Those who fear You will be glad when they
see me, because I have hoped in Your
word ... My soul faints for Your salvation,
but I hope in Your word.
—Psalm 119:74, 81

Blessed is the man who trusts in the Lord,
and whose hope is the Lord
for he shall be like a tree planted by waters, which
spreads out its roots by the river; and
will not fear when heat comes; but its leaf will
be green, and will not be anxious in
the year of drought, nor will cease from yielding fruit.
—Jeremiah 17:7–8

This I recall to my mind, therefore have I
hope ... The Lord is my portion, saith

my soul; therefore, will I hope in Him …
It is good that a man should both
hope and quietly wait for the salvation of the Lord.
—Lamentations 3:21, 24, 26

Who, contrary to hope, in hope believed, so
that he [Abraham] became the father
of many nations, according to what was spoken,
so shall your descendants be, and not being
weak in faith, he did not consider his own
body, already dead (since he was about
a hundred years old), and the deadness of Sarah's womb.
—Romans 4:18–19

And we know that all things work together
for good to them that love God
to them who are the called according to His purpose.
—Romans 8:28

Now may the God of hope fill you with all
joy and peace in believing, that
you may abound in hope by the power of the Holy Spirit.
—Romans 15:13

GOD'S PROMISES FOR DELIVERANCE AND VICTORY

God is our refuge and strength. A very present help in trouble. Therefore, we will not fear, even though the earth be removed, and though the mountains be carried into the midst of the sea. Though its waters roar and be troubled, though the mountains shake with its swelling. Selah.
—Psalm 46:1–3

The Lord shall preserve you from all evil; He shall preserve your soul. The Lord shall preserve your going out and your coming in from this forth, and even forevermore.
—Psalm 121:7–8

Offer to God thanksgiving, and pay your vows to the Most High. Call upon Me [the Lord] in the day of trouble I will deliver you, and you shall glorify Me.
—Psalm 50:14–15

Fear not, for I am with you; be not dismayed, for I am your God, I will strengthen You, Yes, I will help you, I will uphold you with My righteous right hand.
—Isaiah 41:10

No weapon formed against you shall prosper,
and every tongue which rises
against you in judgment You shall condemn.
This is the heritage of the servants
of the Lord, and their righteousness is from Me, says the Lord.
—Isaiah 54:17

Yet in all these things we are more than
conquerors through Him who loved us.
For I am persuaded that neither death nor life, nor angels nor
principalities nor powers, nor things present nor things to come,
nor height nor depth, nor any other created thing, shall be able to
separate us from the love of God which is in Christ Jesus our Lord.
—Romans 8:37–39

GOD'S PROMISES FOR TRUSTING HIM

Our soul waiteth for the Lord; He is our help and our shield.
For our heart shall rejoice in Him, because
we have trusted in His holy name.
—Psalm 33:20–21

This poor man cried out, and the Lord heard him, and saved
him out of all his troubles.... Oh, taste and see that the Lord is good
blessed is the man who trusts in Him [God]!
—Psalm 34:6, 8

In You, O Lord, I put my trust; let me
never be put to shame. Deliver me
in Your righteousness, and cause me to escape.
Incline Your ear to me, and save me.
Be my strong refuge to which I may resort
continually; You have given the
commandment to save me, for You are my rock and my fortress.
—Psalm 71:1–3

For the Lord God is a sun and shield; the
Lord will give grace and glory
no good thing will He withhold from those who walk uprightly ...
O Lord of hosts, blessed is the man who trusts in You!
—Psalm 84:11–12

Trust in the Lord with all your heart, and
lean not on your own understanding
In all your ways acknowledge Him, and He shall direct your paths.
—Proverbs 3:5–6

For I know the thoughts that I think toward
you, says the Lord, thoughts of peace
and not evil, to give you a future and a hope. Then
you will call upon Me and go and pray
to Me, and I will listen to you, and you
will seek Me and find Me, when
you search for Me with all your heart.
—Jeremiah 29:11–13

God's Promises for Security and Peace

The Lord bless you and keep you; the Lord make His face shine
upon you and be gracious to you; the Lord lift up His countenance
upon you, and give you peace.
—Numbers 6:24–26

The Lord is my light and my salvation;
whom shall I fear? The Lord is
the strength of my life; of whom shall I be afraid...
Wait on the Lord; be of good courage
and He shall strengthen your heart; wait, I say, on the Lord.
—Psalm 27:1, 14

You will keep him in perfect peace, whose mind is stayed on You.
Because he trusts in You. Trust in the Lord
forever. For in Yah, the Lord
is everlasting strength ... Lord you will establish peace for us.
For you have also done all our works in us.
—Isaiah 26:3–4, 12

Peace I leave with you, My peace I give to
you, not as the world gives do I give
to you. Let not your heart be troubled, neither let it be afraid.
—John 14:27

But now in Christ Jesus, you who once were
[so] far away, through (by, in) the
blood of Christ have been brought near. For He [Christ] is
[Himself] our peace (our bond of unity and harmony), He
has made us both [Jew and Gentile] one [body], and has
broken down (destroyed, abolished) the
hostile dividing wall between us.
—Ephesians 2:13–14 (AMP)

Don't worry about anything; instead, pray
about everything. Tell God what you
need and thank him for all he has done. If you
do this you will experience God's peace
which is far more wonderful than the human
mind can understand. His peace
will guard your hearts and minds as you live in Christ Jesus.
—Philippians 4:6–7 (NLT)

GOD'S PROMISES FOR REST AND RESTORATION

The Lord is my shepherd; I shall not want,
He makes me to lie down in
green pastures; He leads me beside the still
waters, He restores my soul; He leads
me in the paths of righteousness for His name's sake.
—Psalm 23:1–3

Create in me a clean heart, O God, and renew
a steadfast spirit within me, do not
cast me away from Your presence, and do not
take Your Holy Spirit from me. Restore to
me the joy of Your salvation, and uphold
me by Your generous Spirit.
—Psalm 51:10–12

For I will restore health to you and heal you of
your wounds, says the Lord, because
they called you an outcast saying; this is Zion; no one seeks her.
—Jeremiah 30:17

Come to Me, all you who labor and are heavy laden and
overburdened, and I will cause you to rest [I will ease and relieve
and refresh your souls]. Take My yoke upon you and learn of
Me, for I am gentle (meek) and humble (lowly) in heart, and

you will find rest (relief and ease and refreshment and blessed
quiet) for your souls. For My yoke is wholesome, gracious
and pleasant), and My burden is light and easy to be borne."
—Matthew 11:28–30 (AMP)

So repent (change your mind and purpose); turn around and return
[to God], that your sins may be erased (blotted out, wiped clean),
that times of refreshing (of recovering from the effects of heat, of
reviving with fresh air) may come from the presence of the Lord.
—Acts 3:19 (AMP)

For if Joshua had given them rest, then He
would not afterward have spoken of
another day. There remains therefore a rest for the people
of God. For he who has entered his rest has himself
also ceased from his works as God did from His. Let us
therefore be diligent to enter that rest, lest anyone fall
according to the same example of disobedience.
—Hebrews 4:8–11

GOD'S PROMISES FOR PURPOSE AND FUTURE PLANS

For I know the thoughts that I think toward you, says the Lord
thoughts of peace and not of evil, to give you a future and a hope.
—Jeremiah 29:11

By this My Father is glorified, that you bear much fruit ... You
did not choose Me, but I chose you and appointed you that you
should go and bear fruit, and that your fruit should remain
that whatever you ask the Father in My name He may give you.
—John 15:8, 16

For we are God's [own] handiwork (His workmanship),
recreated in Christ Jesus, [born anew] that we may do those
good works which God predestined (planned beforehand)
for us [taking paths which He prepared ahead of time),
that we should walk in them [living the good life which
He prearranged and made ready for us to live].
—Ephesians 2:10 (AMP)

For God is not unrighteous to forget or overlook your
labor and the love which you have shown for His
name's sake in ministering to the needs of the saints
(His own consecrated people), as you still do.
—Hebrews 6:10 (AMP)

And may the God of peace Himself sanctify you through and through [separate you from profane things, make you pure and wholly consecrate to God]; and may your spirit and soul and body be preserved sound and complete [and found] blameless at the coming of our Lord Jesus Christ (the Messiah), faithful is He Who is calling you [to Himself] and utterly trustworthy and He will also do it [fulfill His call by hallowing and keeping you].
—1 Thessalonians 5:23–24 (AMP)

Therefore, we also pray always for you that our God would count you worthy of this calling, and fulfill all the good pleasure of His goodness and the work of faith with power, that the name of our Lord Jesus Christ may be glorified in you, and you in Him according to the grace of our God and the Lord Jesus Christ.
—2 Thessalonians 1:11–12

God's Promises for Direction and Guidance

And He [God] said, My presence will go with you, and I will give you rest. The he [Moses] said to Him, if Your Presence does not go with us, do not bring us up from here......So the Lord said to Moses, I will also do this thing that you have spoken; for you have found grace in My sight, and I know you by name.
—Exodus 33:14–15, 17

Lean on, trust in, and be confident in the Lord with all your heart and mind and do not rely on your own insight and understanding. In all your ways know, recognize, and acknowledge Him, and He will direct and make straight and plain your paths.
—Proverbs 3:5–6 (AMP)

The Lord is my Shepherd; I shall not want. He makes me to lie down in green pastures; He leads me beside the still waters. He restores my soul; He leads me in the paths of righteousness for His name's sake.
—Psalm 23:1–3

In You, O Lord, I put my trust; let me never be ashamed; deliver me in Your righteousness … For You are my rock and my fortress; therefore, for Your name's sake, lead me and guide me.
—Psalm 31:1, 3

Your word is a lamp to my feet and a light to my
path ... The entrance of Your words gives light; it gives
understanding to the simple ... Direct my steps by Your
word, and let no iniquity have dominion over me.
—Psalm 119:105, 130, 133

I am the good shepherd; and I know My sheep,
and am known by My own ... My sheep hear My
voice, and I know them, and they follow Me.
—John 10:14, 27

GOD'S PROMISES FOR PROVISION AND PERSONAL NEEDS

The LORD is my shepherd [to feed, guide, and shield me],
I shall not lack. He makes me lie down in [fresh, tender]
green pastures He leads me besides the still restful waters.
—Psalm 23:1–2 (AMP)

I have been young, and now am old, yet I have not seen the
righteous forsaken, nor His descendants begging bread. He
is ever merciful, and lends and his descendants are blessed.
—Psalm 37:25–26

And GOD is able to make all grace (every favor and earthly
blessing) come to you in abundance, so that you may always and
under all circumstances and whatever the need be self-sufficient
[possessing enough to require no aid or support and furnished
in abundance for every good work and charitable donation].
—2 Corinthians 9:8

And my GOD shall supply all your need according
to His riches in glory by Christ Jesus. Now to our
GOD and Father be glory and ever. Amen.
—Philippians 4:19–20

Grace and peace be multiplied to you in the knowledge of GOD
and of Jesus our Lord, as His divine power has given to us all
things that pertain to life and godliness through the knowledge

of Him who called us by glory and virtue by which have been given to us exceedingly great and precious promises ...
—2 Peter 1:2–4

Now this is the confidence that we have in Him, that if we ask anything according to His will, He hears us. And if we know that He hears us, whatever we ask we know that we have the petitions that we have asked of Him.
—1 John 5:14–15

GOD'S PROMISES FOR SAFETY AND PROTECTION

He who dwells in the secret place of the Most High
shall remain stable and fixed under the shadow of the
Almighty [Whose power no foe can withstand].

I will say of the Lord, He is my refuge and my fortress, my God
on Him I lean and rely, and in Him I [confidently] trust!

For [then] He will deliver you from the snare of
the fowler and from the deadly pestilence.

[Then] He will cover you with His pinions, and under
His wings shall you trust and find refuge; His truth
and His faithfulness are a shield and a buckler.

[I] shall not be afraid of the terror of the night, nor of the arrow
(the evil plots and slanders of the wicked) that flies by day.

Nor of the pestilence that stalks in darkness, nor of the destruction
and sudden death that surprise and lay waste at noonday.

A thousand may fall at [my] side, and ten thousand at
[my] right hand but it shall not come near [me].

Only a specular shall [I] be [inaccessible in the secret place of
the Most High] as you witness the reward of the wicked.

Because [I] have made the Lord my refuge, and
the Most High my dwelling place.

There shall no evil befall [me], nor any plague
of calamity come near [my] tent.

For He [God] will give His angels {especial] charge
over [me] to accompany and defend and preserve [me]
in all [my] ways [of obedience and service].

They shall bear [me] up on their hands, lest
[I] dash [my] foot against a stone.

[I] shall tread upon the lion and adder; the young
lion and the serpent shall [I] trample underfoot.

Because [I] have set my love upon [God], therefore will
[He] deliver [me]; [God] will set [me] on high, because I
know and understand [His] name [has a personal knowledge
of [His] mercy, love, and kindness—trusts and relies on
[His], knowing I will never forsake [me], no never].

[I] shall call upon [Him], and [He] will answer [me]; [He] will
be with me in trouble, [He] will deliver [me] and honor [me].

With long life will [He] satisfy [me] and show [me] [His] salvation.
—Psalm 91:1–16

I cried to the LORD with my voice, and He heard me
from His holy hill. I lay down and slept; I awoke, for the
LORD sustained me. I will not be afraid of ten thousands
of people who have set themselves against me all around.
—Psalm 3:4–6

There are many who say, who will show us any good? LORD,
lift up the light of Your countenance upon us, You have

put gladness in my heart. More than in the season that their grain and wine increased. I will both lie down in peace, and sleep. For You alone, O LORD make me dwell in safety.
—Psalm 4:6–8

I have called upon You, for You will hear me, O GOD; Incline Your ear to me and hear my speech, show Your marvelous lovingkindness by Your right hand, O You who save those who trust in You, from those who rise up against them, keep me as the apple of Your eye. Hide me under the shadow of Your wings, from the wicked who oppress me, from my deadly enemies who surround me.
—Psalm 17:6–8

I sought the LORD, and He heard me, and delivered me from all my fears. They looked me from and were radiant, and their faces were not ashamed. This poor man cried out, and the LORD heard him, and saved him out of all his troubles. The angel of the LORD encamps all around those who fear Him, and delivers them.
—Psalm 14:4–7

But I will sing of Your power; Yes, I will sing aloud of Your mercy in the for You have been my defense and refuge in the day of my trouble. To You, O my strength I will sing praises. For GOD is my defense, my GOD of mercy.
—Psalm 59:16–17

GOD'S PROMISES FOR FAITHFULNESS

Therefore, know that the Lord your God, He is God, the faithful
God who keeps covenant and mercy for a thousand generations
with those who love Him and keep His commandments.
—Deuteronomy 7:9

I have not hidden Your righteousness within my heart; I have
declared Your faithfulness and Your salvation; I have not concealed
Your lovingkindness and Your truth from the great assembly.
—Psalm 40:10

But remember that the temptations that come into your life are
no different from what others experience. And God is faithful,
He will keep the temptations from becoming so strong that
you can't stand up against them. When you are tempted He
will show you a way out so that you will not give in to it.
—1 Corinthians 10:12–13 (NLT)

Finally, brethren pray for us that the word of the Lord
may run swiftly and be glorified, just as it is with you, and
that we may be delivered from unreasonable and wicked
men, for not all have faith. But the Lord is faithful, who
will establish you and guard you from the evil one.
—2 Thessalonians 3:1–3

Therefore, in all things He had to be made like His brethren
that He might be a merciful and faithful High Priest in things
pertaining to God to make propitiation for the sins of the people.
—Hebrews 2:17

Therefore, brethren having boldness to enter the
Holiness by the blood of Jesus, by a new and living way
which He consecrated for us, through the veil, that is
His flesh ... Let us hold fast the confession of our hope
without wavering, for He who promised is faithful.
—Hebrews 10:19–20; 23

GOD'S PROMISES FOR LISTENING, FOLLOWING, AND APPLYING HIS WORD

The Word of God will produce faith.
So then faith comes by hearing, and hearing by the word of God.
—Romans 10:17

The Word of God is the seed of the new birth.
Of His own will He brought us forth by the word of truth, that we
might be a kind of firstfruits of His creatures.
—James 1:18

The Word of God provides spiritual nourishment.
But He [Jesus] answered and said, it is written,
man shall not live by bread alone
but by every word that proceeds from the mouth of God.
—Matthew 4:4

The Word of God spiritual illumination.
Your testimonies are wonderful; therefore,
my soul keeps them. The entrance of
Your words gives light; it gives understanding to the simple.
—Psalm 119:130

The Word of God provides physical healing.
My son, give attention to my words, incline
your ear to my sayings. Do not let
them depart from your eyes; keep them in
the midst of your heart; for they
are life to those who find them, and health to all their flesh.
—Proverbs 4:20–22

The Word of God makes possible victory
over Satan and sin when we apply it.
How can a young man cleanse his way? By taking
heed according to Your word ... Your
word have hidden [stored up] in my heart,
that I might not sin against You.
—Psalm 119–9, 11

The Word of God provides spiritual cleansing and sanctification.
Husbands, love your wives, just as Christ also loves the church
and gave Himself for he that He might sanctify and cleanse her
with the washing of water by the word, that He night present her
to Himself a glorious church, not having spot or wrinkle or any
such thing, but that she should be holy and without blemish.
—Ephesians 5:25–27

The Word of God is a spiritual mirror..
Therefore, putting aside all filthiness and all that remains of
wickedness, in humility receive the word implanted, which is
able to save your souls. But prove yourselves doers of the word,
and not merely hearers who delude themselves. For if anyone is
a hearer of the and not a doer, he is like a man who looks at his
natural face in a mirror; for once he has looked at himself and
gone away, he has immediately forgotten what kind of person
he was. But one who looks intently at the perfect law of liberty,

and abides by it, not having become a forgetful hearer but an effectual doer, this man shall be blessed in what he does.
—James 1:21–25 (NASB)

The Word of God provides a spiritual weapon
against the assaults of the devil.
Stand therefore, and having girded your waste with truth, having put on the breastplate of righteousness, and having shod your feet with the preparation of the gospel of peace; above all, taking the shield of faith with which you will I be able to quench all the fiery darts of the wicked one. And take the helmet of salvation, and the sword of the Spirit, which is the word of God.
—Ephesians 6:14–17

The Word of God is our ultimate judge.
And if any one hears My sayings, and does not keep them, I do not judge him for I did not come to judge the world, but to save the world. He who rejects Me, and does not receive My saying, has one who judges him; the word I spoke is what will judge him at the last day.
—John 12:47–48 (NASB)

✧ ✧ ✧

And this is the confidence (the assurance, the privilege of boldness) which we have in Him; [we are sure] that if we ask anything (make any request) according to His will (in agreement with His own plan); He listens to and hears us. And if (since) we [positively] know that He listens to us in whatever we ask we also know [with settled and absolute knowledge] that we have [granted us as our present possessions] the requests made of Him.

—1 John 5:14–15 (AMP)

SECTION 3

✧✧✧

PRAYERS, PETITIONS, AND SPIRITUAL WARFARE PRAYERS

A Pattern for Bold, Fervent Prayers When Confronted with Spiritual Attacks and Life's Adversities

EFFECTUAL FERVENT
PRAYERS

Let's us then fearlessly and confidently and boldly draw near
to the throne of grace (the throne of God's unmerited favor
to us sinners), that we may receive mercy [for our failures] and
find grace to help in good time for every need [appropriate
help and well-timed help, coming just when we need it] ...
The earnest (heartfelt, continued) prayer of a righteous man
makes tremendous power available [dynamic in its working].
—Hebrews 4:16; James 5:16 (AMP)

Prayer is one of the greatest opportunities, one of the greatest
privileges, and one of the greatest ministries available to all Christians.
But there are many Spirit-filled believers who struggle with prayer.
They either don't take time to pray or simply don't know how to
pray. What's even more, many have given up on praying or have
become discouraged in prayer. But Jesus said, "Men always ought
to pray and not lose heart" (Luke 18:1). We must draw fearlessly and
boldly before the throne of grace because it brings salvation, healing,
and deliverance.

Our Heavenly Father hears the prayers of those who call upon
Him. (See Psalm 65:2.) The Father not only welcomes prayer but
also delights in answering our prayers. His willingness and ability to
answer our prayers is "exceedingly abundantly above all that we ask
or think ..." (Ephesians 3:20). The late John Wesley that wrote in
his journal, "I am persuaded that God does everything by prayer and
nothing without it." What Mr. Wesley wrote is accurate and Biblical,
because Paul wrote "Be anxious for nothing, but in everything by

prayer and supplication, with thanksgiving, let your requests be made known to God" (Philippians 4:6).

Proverbs 18:21 says, "Death and life are in the power of the tongue," so it's important we incorporate the Word of God into our prayers. This is why we should read, study, and meditate on the Scriptures. Because when we confess and proclaim God's Word, we're speaking life into our circumstances. God honors His Word. Remember: God said His thoughts are not our thoughts, nor our ways His ways, but proclaiming God's Word in prayer unveils and releases His thoughts and will about a situation or circumstance. (See Isaiah 55:8.)

> The earnest (heartfelt, continued) prayer of a righteous man makes tremendous power available [dynamic in its working]. Elijah was a human being with a nature such as we have [with feelings, affections, and a constitution like ours]; and he prayed earnestly for it not to rain, and no rain fell on the earth for three years and six months. And [then] he prayed again and the heavens supplied rain and the land produced its crops [as usual]. (James 5:16–17 AMP)

It was Peter who said, "In truth I perceive that God shows no partiality" (Acts 10:34). In other words, similar to how Elijah prayed, we, too, can receive answers to prayer. Through prayer, supernatural power is available to us. I must point out that Elijah was an anointed prophet, but the Bible is careful to mention that He was just like we are. (See James 5:17.) But there's one very important thing that sets great men and women apart from the normal average saint: effectual fervent prayer. Following are a couple of examples of this:

> In World War 1, Howard was a conscientious objector and wound up in prison because of it. The prison was a damp, leaky place. He was lying in bed one day and a little stream of water was trickling down from the

ceiling and splashing over him. He pointed his finger at it and said, "I command you to go back, in the name of Jesus" and it did ... Here is another story. In Zambia, a teenage African girl was bicycling to the place where we were holding a meeting. They have vast anthills in Zambia—twenty or thirty feet high—and they are home to snakes. As she approached an anthill, a big black cobra came out its hole toward her. She came to a stop on her bicycle, trembling terribly. But then the Spirit of God came upon her, and she said, "In the name of the Lord Jesus Christ, go back into your hole." The cobra stopped and turned its head toward the hole, but it remained motionless. She spoke again; "No, I said go back into your hole." At that, it turned around and went right back in. When she got to our meeting place she was still trembling. In that command God's strength was made perfect in weakness. [15]

In both examples, the man and girl prayed using verbal utterance and authority. For instance, the teenage girl spoke to her mountain (the snake), invoking Jesus's name. At the command of Jesus's name, the snake had no choice but to go back to where it came from. But it wasn't her voice that got the cobra's attention but the name of the Lord Jesus Christ. Whatever we encounter in life, we must employ the instrument of prayer and invoke the name of Jesus. By doing so, we're casting all our care upon Him. (See 1 Peter 5:7.)

When it comes to spiritual warfare, our fight is not with human beings but with the kingdom of darkness (devil and his demons). Satan's objective is to silence the gospel by attempting to defeat us through strategies and deception. Remember: Jesus said that he is "a murderer from the beginning, and does not stand in the truth, because there is no truth in him. When He speaks a lie, he speaks from his own resources, for he is a liar and the father of it" (John 8:44). In order to defeat the enemy, we must recognize the battle is not with flesh and blood. Ephesians 6:12 says, "For we do not wrestle against flesh and blood, but against principalities, against powers, against the rulers of the darkness of this age, against spiritual hosts of wickedness in the heavenly places."

Now that we fully understand that our battles are not with flesh and blood, we must use the weapon of prayer. David understood the importance of prayer in the many battles he faced. In many psalms he wrote, he often prayed for the defeat of his enemies, and God answered. God is not a respecter of persons. We can experience that same victory over our spiritual enemies. But we must always remember that we're not fighting against flesh and blood but against principalities, powers, rulers of darkness, and a host of wickedness.

Prayer is also effective for eradicating strongholds. A stronghold is a pattern or idea that governs individuals, nations, and communities. It is a mindset or thought pattern that causes people to act, react, and respond in a negative manner that's contrary to God's ways and His Word. There are multitudes of people who are deceived by the enemy. Given that the weapons of our warfare are not carnal, we can "Cast down arguments and every high thing that exalts itself against the knowledge of God, bringing every thought into captivity to the obedience of Christ" (2 Corinthians 10:5). When we pray fervently, it can strip the strongholds of deceiving spirits and release people from every form of bondage.

Praying according to God's will helps us pray with confidence. First John 5:14–15 says, "Now this is the confidence that we have in Him, that if we ask anything according to His will, He hears us, and if we know that He hears us, whatever we ask, we know that we have the petitions we have asked of Him." When we have full knowledge and understanding of God, the result will always be effective prayer. We can walk with confidence knowing we received what we asked for. The following are suggested prayer patterns we can pray for various circumstances and when engaged in spiritual warfare.

Prayer Pattern for the Spirit of Rejection

Father, I come before You in the name of Jesus Christ, I believe that You are the Son of God and the only way to the Father. I believe You died on the cross for my sins and iniquities and that You rose again from the dead. Lord, I repent of all my sins, and just as You have forgiven me, I forgive everyone, including those who have rejected me, hurt me, betrayed me, and failed to show me love. I ask that You forgive me.

Lord Jesus, I believe that You have not rejected me and that because of what You did for me on the cross I am accepted. Because of the atonement, I am highly favored; I am the object of Your special care, compassion, and love. Lord Jesus, Your Father is my Father, and heaven is my home. I am a member of the family of God—the best family in the world. Thank You so much!

Lord Jesus, I accept myself the way You have wonderfully and fearfully made me. I am Your created workmanship, and I thank You for what You have done. You have begun a good work in me, and You will bring it to completion when my life ends and You call me home.

Now, Lord Jesus, I proclaim and declare my complete release from any dark evil spirit that has exploited and taken advantage of the wounds in my life. I release my spirit to rejoice in You. Lord Jesus, I ask all of this in Your precious name. Amen!

Prayer Pattern for Divine Protection

Father, in the name of Jesus, thank You for divine protection. I ask You to keep a hedge of protection around me, my family, my loved ones, my mind, my heart, my ministry, my church, and my relationship with You.

Father, the same hedge of protection You put around Your servants throughout the Bible, I ask You to keep it around all that pertains to me. Thank You for an encampment of angels surrounding me and my loved ones, my ministry, and my church every moment of the day.

Father, I thank You that no weapon that has been formed shall prosper and that every tongue that has risen in judgment You shall condemn. I thank You that I can cast every care I have upon You, for You care for me. Heal and strengthen me, and forgive those who have allowed the enemy to use them against me.

Father, let Your glory be my rear guard. I ask in the name of Jesus that You surround me and my loved ones with a supernatural defense barrier, a supernatural wall of fire. Father, protect me and my loved ones from the assaults of the kingdom of darkness. I receive and claim Your promise to be my shield and protector each and every day. I ask all of these things in the mighty name of Jesus. Amen!

Prayer Pattern for False Religion and Practices

Father, in the name of Jesus, I renounce and repent of, and break free from, religious tradition, false beliefs, false practices, legalism, formalism, cessationism, self-righteousness, doctrines of demons, dogmatism, atheism, and any form of bondage.

Additionally, I renounce the worship of false gods, the worship of Mary, the worship of men and women, the worship of angels, idolatry, rites, creeds, and ritual and unholy alliances. Father, You said that whom the Son has set free is free indeed. I ask all of this in Jesus's name. Amen!

Prayer Pattern for Divine Protection and Deliverance

Father, I come before You in Jesus's name. I believe no weapon that has beenformed against me and my family shall prosper, and every tongue that has risen against me in judgment I do condemn. Father, if there are those who have been speaking or praying against me, or trying to harm me, I forgive them. Having forgiven them, I bless them in the name of the Lord.

Lord, I confess that You alone are my God and my Lord and Savior, and beside You there is no other. I praise You; I worship You, and I fully surrender to Your Lordship in complete obedience. I am submitted to Your Word; I obey Your Word. Having submitted to Your Word, I resist the devil and all His attacks, pressures, deceptions, lies, and every instrument or agent he would seek to use against me and my loved one. Father, I ask all of this in Jesus's name. Amen!

PRAYER PATTERN FOR DIVINE HEALING AND HEALTH

Father, I come before You in Jesus's name. Lord, I believe that Your atoning work at the cross has paved the way for my physical healing and health. According to the Bible, You have taken my infirmities and borne my sicknesses. Thank You for not allowing any sickness and disease to come near my dwelling.

Lord, I thank You for healing every part of my physical frame. I am healed by the stripes of Jesus Christ! Thank You, Lord, for healing me of hypertension, fear, and anxiety. Thank You, Lord, for healing my muscles, joints, kidneys, heart, bladder, spine, back breast, sinuses, lungs, legs, and feet, in the name of Jesus!

Lord, thank You for healing of me of diabetes, multiple sclerosis, rheumatoid arthritis, every form of cancer, high cholesterol, a weakened immune system, blood disease, lupus, Alzheimer's, sleep disorders, asthma, breathing disorders, bone disease, and every form of sickness and disease, in Jesus's name. Amen!

Prayer Pattern for Spiritual Warfare

Father, I come in the name of Jesus! According to Your Word, I believe no weapon formed against me shall prosper. Lord, You came not only to save us from our sins but also to destroy the works of the devil. Lord, lift up a standard against any flood the enemy would try to bring into my life. You said that whatsoever we bind on earth, so it is bound in heaven.

Father, I bind and cast out any demonic thief that would try to steal my joy and peace, in the name of Jesus. Father, I bind and cast out demonic spirits that would attack me, my family, my ministry, and my loved ones, in the name of Jesus.

Father, I bind and rebuke any demon that would attempt to block and hinder my spiritual progress, any ministry endeavors, and the work of the kingdom. Father, I block and bind any deceiving and seducing spirits that would try to enter my life.

Father, deliver me and my loved ones out of the hands of wicked, ungodly,

unreasonable men and women. Father, I thank You for delivering me from the snare of the fowler and from perilous pestilence. You are My refuge and fortress, and Your truth is My shield and buckler.

Father, dismantle every evil work of witchcraft in my region and state. Lord, destroy every wicked cauldron in my city. Lord, visit every witch, warlock, medium, and witch doctor in my region, city, state, and nation. Let them repent, turn to You, and be saved.

Father, I thank You for covering me with the blood of Jesus. Because of the atoning work of Christ, I triumph and am more than a conqueror through Him. Father, I thank You because Satan was defeated at the cross. I overcome him by the blood of the Lamb and the word of my testimony. Father, I ask all of this in Jesus's name. Amen!

Prayer Pattern for Breaking Generational Curses

Lord Jesus Christ, I believe that You are the Son of
God and the only way to God: and that You died on
the cross for my sins and rose again from the dead.

I give up all my rebellion and all my sin, and
I submit myself to You as My Lord.

I confess all my sins before You and ask for Your forgiveness—
especially for any sins that exposed me to a curse. Release
me also, from the consequences of my ancestors' sins.

By a decision of my will, I forgive all who have
harmed me or wronged me—just as I want God to
forgive me. In particular, I forgive..........

I renounce all contact with anything occult or satanic—
if I have any "contact objects" I commit myself to
destroy them. I cancel all Satan's claims against me.

Lord Jesus, I believe that on the cross You took on Yourself every
curse that could ever come upon me. So I ask You now to release
me from every curse over my life—in Your name, Lord Jesus
Christ! By faith I now receive my release and I thank You for it.[16]

Prayer Pattern for Receiving God's Grace Instead of Working

Dear Father, I come to You in the name of Your Son, the Lord Jesus, I confess that I have tried to earn Your blessings and favor by own efforts. I have tried to attain a personal standard of righteousness that I thought would make me acceptable to You. I ask forgiveness in the name of Jesus. Would You please deliver me from any form of darkness that has surrounded me because of the curse of the broken law!

I humble myself before You, and I confess that I am receiving Your grace and favor by faith. I make the decision to stop working for Your favor. And I humbly declare that I am righteous before You, not based on anything I have done, but on the righteousness of Christ, which has been given me based on His finished work on the cross on my behalf, I confess that it is a free gift, not bestowed upon me because of any righteousness or merit on my part.

I ask that throughout my life You would, by Your Holy Spirit, enlighten me whenever I begin to rely on my own strength and efforts to live righteously before You. I ask that in my times of need You would grant me the understanding always to turn to the graces that are in the fullness of Christ to overcome the sins and weaknesses in my life. I declare that I trust in Your grace alone to walk with Christ.

Thank You for the grace You have granted me. Thank You for the grace that has called me into Jesus, forgiven me of every sin. Justified me by His work, made me alive by His Spirit and raised me up with Him to sit in heavenly places. Thank You for Your grace which is always sufficient for all my needs for all of my life. Now Father, help me as I go forward in Your grace, of other with the power of Your grace. In Jesus' name, Amen![17]

Prayer Pattern for Salvation

Lord God, thank You for sending Your son, Jesus, to suffer and die for me. I know that without Him I would be separated from You forever. I confess and repent of all my sins. I receive You, Jesus, into my heart and life as my personal Lord and Savior. Lord Jesus, baptize me with the Holy Spirit so that I can serve and live for You. Lord, help me find a church or ministry in which I may grow in grace. Now take full control of my life in the name of Jesus. Amen!

TOPIC INDEX

proclaiming the Word 171, 306

loneliness, fear
debilitating strongman 95
epidemic of loneliness 57
loneliness exacerbated 231

love, unity
accepted in the beloved 5, 51, 52, 278
epidemic of loneliness 57
Abba Father 79
impartation of love 197
incredible memory 31
love in action 253
reerected walls 193
striving for love 159
unconditional love 67, 80

miracles, supernatural
able and willing xxi, 26, 34, 37, 39, 44
always on time 13, 14, 60, 71, 300
bore our sicknesses 127, 177, 317
breakthrough prayers 77
desperate measures 125
faith, not sight 45
faith to be healed 225
God still speaks 169
humankind's inability, God's opportunity 9
Jehovah-Rapha 23, 178
manufacturer's warranty 43, 44
no partiality 37, 193, 260, 348

supernatural attestation 259
touched him 27, 255
Syrophoenician woman 299
proclaiming the Word 171, 306

power of the tongue
don't receive the mail 49
effective communicator 285
gracious words 73, 286
grieving friend 251
don't receive the mail 49

praise and worship
continual praise 53
garment of praise 85, 86
soul blessing 221
weapons of praise 69

protection, security
the Comforter 181
divine protection 279, 280, 352, 354
He rescues 81, 82
not my battle 133
total protection 161

provision
salt of the earth 223, 224
fishers of men 217, 218
ordered steps 195
provision for the purpose 123

restitution, restoration
God of second chances 110
grace to get up 191
joy of salvation 101, 189
reset 121, 122

restitution 189, 190
rolled away 129

salvation
amazing grace 103, 370
come to Jesus 102, 297
extraordinarily patient 215
finished work 52, 127, 128,
274, 359
heart faith 185, 186
joy of salvation 101, 189
religion or relationship 199
the way, truth, and door 15

spiritual bondage, legalism, religious tradition
blessings and curses i, 243
come to Jesus 102, 297
Egypt or Promised Land 283
Hagar and Sarah 35
His yoke is easy 204, 211
new wine and old wineskins
203
pharisaism (self-righteousness)
265
righteousness that exceeds
257
root problems i, 271
unhealthy co-dependency
111
yoke of bondage 29, 30

spiritual growth, identity
adversity to purpose 83
come to Jesus 102, 297
effects of God's Word 291
Egypt or Promised Land 283

leaving elementary principles
267
man of valor 139
room to grow 141
spiritual metamorphosis 227
spiritual orphans 145, 179
thoroughly equipped 213,
247, 291, 314

spiritual promises, benefits
the Administrator 293
better covenant 8, 29, 36, 113,
147, 273, 274
better promises 8, 29, 36, 147
bore our sicknesses 127, 177,
317
finished work 52, 127, 128,
274, 359
no hidden clauses 113
remember His benefits 91

spiritual warfare
the battlefield 205
breakthrough prayers 77
different outlook 201
keys of the kingdom 175, 176
blood of the lamb 10, 173,
262, 309, 357
don't receive the mail 49
midnight need 107
not my battle 133
persistence 41, 42, 78, 107,
215, 263
weapons of praise 69
proclaiming the Word 171,
306

NOTES

1   Partial lyrics to "God Will Take Care of You" taken from *Sing His Praise* by Gospel Publishing House Copyright © 1991 by Gospel Publishing House. Used with permission from My Healthy Church.

2   Partial lyrics to "Through It All" taken from *Sing His Praise* by Gospel Publishing House Copyright © 1991 by Gospel Publishing House. Used with permission from My Healthy Church.

3   Craig Brian Larson, *750 Engaging Illustrations for Preachers, Teachers & Writers* (Ada, Michigan: Baker Books, 2002), 419.

4   Partial lyrics to "He Is Jehovah" taken from *Sing His Praise* by Gospel Publishing House Copyright © 1991 by Gospel Publishing House. Used with permission from My Healthy Church.

5   Partial lyrics to "Jesus Never Fails" taken from Sing His Praise by Gospel Publishing House Copyright © 1991 by Gospel Publishing House. Used with permission from My Healthy Church.

6   Craig Brian Larson, *750 Engaging Illustrations for Preachers, Teachers & Writers* (Ada, Michigan: Baker Books, 2002), 334

7   Craig Brian Larson, *750 Engaging Illustrations for Preachers, Teachers & Writers* (Ada, Michigan: Baker Books, 2002), 58

8   Partial lyrics to "Standing On the Promises" taken from *Sing His Praise* by Gospel Publishing House Copyright © 1991 by Gospel Publishing House. Used with permission from My Healthy Church.

9   Partial lyrics to "Amazing Grace" taken from *Sing His Praise* by Gospel Publishing House Copyright © 1991 by Gospel Publishing House. Used with permission from My Healthy Church.

10 Craig Brian Larson, *750 Engaging Illustrations for Preachers, Teachers & Writers* (Ada, Michigan: Baker Books, 2002), 281

11 Derek Prince, *"How to Find Your Place"* excerpt taken from Derek Prince Legacy Newsletter (Charlotte, North Carolina).

12 Craig Brian Larson, *750 Engaging Illustrations for Preachers, Teachers & Writers* (Ada, Michigan: Baker Books, 2002), 247

13 Partial lyrics to "Love Lifted Me" taken from *Sing His Praise* by Gospel Publishing House Copyright © 1991 by Gospel Publishing House. Used with permission from My Healthy Church.

14 T. D. Jakes, *Can You Stand to Be Blessed?* (Shippensburg, Pennsylvania: Treasure House, 1994), 111.

15 Derek Prince, *Secrets of a Prayer Warrior* (Grand Rapids, Michigan: Chosen Books, 2009), 92.

16 Derek Prince, *Blessing or Curse, You Can Choose,* written by Derek Prince (Grand Rapids, Michigan: Chosen Books, 2007) 216–17.

17 Derek Prince, "By Grace Alone" (Grand Rapids, Michigan: Chosen Books, 2013), 219–20.

GOD'S COMPASSION NEVER FAILS

Notes, Prayers, Prophecies, Dreams, and Visions

✧ ✧ ✧

God's Compassion Never Fails

Notes, Prayers, Prophecies, Dreams, and Visions

✦ ✦ ✦

God's Compassion Never Fails

Notes, Prayers, Prophecies, Dreams, and Visions

✧ ✧ ✧

God's Compassion Never Fails

Notes, Prayers, Prophecies, Dreams, and Visions

✧✧✧

ABOUT THE AUTHOR

Donald Spellman is an apostle and the cofounder of Living Word of Grace Ministries (LWOGM) Inc., a nondenominational ministry. He is an author, writer, apostolic Bible teacher, and former pastor of over twenty-one years, and has been in radio ministry since 1992. Additionally, he's the author of four books (*Christ Still Heals, Words Have Great Power, Freedom from Spiritual Bondage,* and *God's Magnificent Grace*). Spellman was born in Elizabeth City, North Carolina, and graduated in 1982 from Northeastern High School. In 1983, he joined the US armed forces, where he worked in Battalion S-1 Headquarters as a personnel administrative specialist in the US Army until he retired.

After serving in the military, he was diagnosed with cancer and was healed by Christ in 1988. Subsequently, after giving his life to Christ in 1985 and serving as an ordained deacon in Germany, he was called to the ministry in 1989 and later ordained in 1991. After ministering and carrying out the work of an evangelist for a short period in 1992, he and his wife launched and founded LWOGM Inc. In 1995, he joined the US Postal Service, where he worked as a letter carrier until he retired in 2005 to begin full-time ministry.

As a result of serving in the pastorate for over twenty-one years, Apostle Spellman has a burden and compassionate heart for spiritual leaders and for those in the office of ministry. He and his wife operate as an apostolic ministry team. The primary objective of LWOGM and the Healing Ministry Broadcast is to win souls for the kingdom of God.

Another aspect of their ministry is to bring healing and restoration (spiritually, physically, and emotionally) to the body of Christ and to equip the saints for ministry through expository teaching of the Word of God through the work of the Holy Spirit. He and his wife have been married for more than thirty-eight years and reside in Baxley, Georgia. They have four grown sons.

GOD'S COMPASSION NEVER FAILS

Not long ago, my wife and I were visiting my brother Tyrone in the hospital out of town. As we walked down the corridors, I couldn't help but notice many sick and suffering people, especially in the critical ward departments. Understandably, the hospital is where you will find sick and suffering people, but I realize this is how Christ sees suffering humanity. God is greatly in touch and concerned about the suffering and needs of humankind. Ours is a world full of spiritually and physically sick souls. I pray that this devotional book will help those that need assurance, hope, and healing.

God's Compassion Never Fails is a three-part daily devotional book about Christ's willingness to assist in the needs of humankind. Section 1 is devoted to scriptures and devotions. Section 2 contains proclamations and confessions, as well as promises from God. Section 3 has pattern prayers to help you pray about your circumstances. All sections are intended to encourage, inspire, comfort, provide hope, and strengthen faith. After you read and meditate on the contents, pass it along if you desire, or add it to your spiritual library. This book can be used for personal study, Bible studies, small cell groups, or Sunday school classes. It's a great spiritual resource to pick up anytime you're facing life's adversities and difficulties.

◆ ENCOURAGING
   ◆ INSPIRATIONAL
      ◆ COMFORTING
         ◆ PROVIDING HOPE
            ◆ STRENGTHENING FAITH

With a focus on winning souls for the kingdom of God, Apostle Donald Spellman ministers healing and restoration—spiritually, physically, and emotionally—to the body of Christ. Spellman is a spiritual leader, apostolic teacher, writer, author, and host of a weekly radio broadcast. In addition, he is a former pastor of over twenty-two years and a retired military veteran with civil service experience. Along with his wife and cofounder of Living Word of Grace Ministries, Spellman leads an apostolic ministry and resides in Georgia.

Printed in the United States
by Baker & Taylor Publisher Services